Deconstructing Essentialism

Anne-Iris Romens

Deconstructing Essentialism

Migrant Women in Stratified Labour Markets

palgrave
macmillan

Anne-Iris Romens
University of Milan - Bicocca
Milan, Italy

ISBN 978-3-031-14398-4 ISBN 978-3-031-14399-1 (eBook)
https://doi.org/10.1007/978-3-031-14399-1

This Palgrave Macmillan imprint is published by the registered company Springer Nature Switzerland AG.
The registered company address is: Gewerbestrasse 11, 6330 Cham, Switzerland

Acknowledgments

My first thanks go to the 51 participants who accepted to contribute to my research. Thank you for sharing your experience, feelings, and thoughts.

I am specially grateful to Devi Sacchetto, from the University of Padua, for his support all along the process of conducting research and drafting a book. Special thanks also go to Valeria Piro, Thomas Romens, Angela Maria Toffanin, and Francesca Alice Vianello, for their support and the time they have dedicated to my work, proofreading the book, and providing valuable comments. I also thank Valentina Pacetti and Paolo Rossi from the University of Milan Bicocca for their trust and support in conducting research.

I would also like to express my gratitude to all the scholars and friends who have contributed to this work with proofreading, discussions, and facilitating access to participants. More specifically, I thank Eleonore Kofman and Kyoko Shinozaki, as well as Fabienne Bretin, Ligia Camargo, Aby Faye, Ru Gao, Paolo Gusmeroli, Tsara Hilbold, Sandra Agyei Kyeremeh, Abdoulaye Ngom, David Primo, Alessandra Siino, Stéphanie Specht, Isabelle Wilhelm, and the members of Arising Africans, associazione Ebene, association Plurielles and association Rhin-Volga.

I am also grateful to Palgrave's editors and staff, in particular to Alec Selwyn and Liam Inscoe - Jones, for making the project of publishing my research possible and to the anonymous reviewers for their useful comments.

This work would not have been possible without the financial support of the University of Padua and the University of Milan Bicocca.

Finally, I would like to especially thank my family and Alvise, for his patience and support, and a loving thanks to Leo, who often complained about mommy "working too much".

May 2022, Anne-Iris Romens.

Mommy writing in English, Leo.

Contents

List of Tables

List of Schemes

1

Studying Stratifications and Essentialism in the Labour Market

> *I repeated exactly, enunciating the syllables, what I had said: I wanted to practice my social work profession, and I did not want anything else.*
>
> *This time, the counsellor, who, I knew later, was a social worker herself, could not repress her irritation at what she perceived as naivety or, even worse, stubbornness:*
>
> *"But do you know at least what a social worker is? And what path must be followed? You might consider something more accessible to you. Look, since it seems you want to work in this area, you could become a domestic assistant, that's suitable".*
>
> Scholastique Mukasonga (2018: 133)[1]

The experience of Mukasonga's heroine could be that of one of my interviewees. After struggling to obtain her diploma in Burundi, the woman is faced with French social workers and recruiters that give no value to her "so beautiful diploma". Moreover, the employment counsellor advises her to look for a job with low social recognition in the care sector, where the woman will make little use of her educational background and her prior professional experience. Scholastique Mukasonga

[1] My translation.

A.-I. Romens, *Deconstructing Essentialism*,
https://doi.org/10.1007/978-3-031-14399-1_1

gives a literary perspective on the struggles and challenges that migrant women with tertiary education face when looking for employment in their field, and that are at the core of this book.

Although holding tertiary education is expected to facilitate access to rewarding positions (OECD, 2019), returns on education for migrant women are reduced. Regardless of their educational background, migrant women in Western Europe primarily find employment in jobs at the bottom of the employment structure (Kofman, 2012; OECD, 2014; Grigoleit-Richter, 2017). With the same level of education, they tend to perform jobs with lower social recognition and income compared to non-migrant women and men.

Scholars have explored the impact of migration policies (Liversage, 2009; Purkayastha & Bircan, 2021), of low recognition of skills gained abroad (Chiswick & Miller, 2009; Kofman, 2012; Coccia & Pittau, 2016), and of networks (Tognetti Bordogna, 2012) in confining migrant women at the bottom of the employment structure. However, the literature on migrant women with tertiary education, or so-called *skilled* migrations, has given little attention to the influence that essentialism has on limiting access to jobs. Essentialism is a process through which people become defined as a group based on alleged common biological or cultural characteristics (Grosz, 1990). As it will be further explored in the book, essentialism is imposed by a dominant group on an oppressed group, to justify inequality in access to resources, including access to graduate jobs.

In Italy and France, the few publications that have tackled essentialism in the recruitment and selection process, have not especially taken into account migrant women's educational background (Scrinzi, 2013). Conversely, scholars that have studied the paths of migrant women with tertiary education in these countries rarely analyse the impact of essentialism in limiting their access to employment (Brandi, 2010; Killian & Manohar, 2015).

Different factors have contributed to understudying the topic. In European countries, including France and Italy, scholars tend to be reluctant to refer to racialisation as a lens through which to analyse social relations (Lentin, 2014). In France, although debates concerning the racialisation of social relations are finding their way into academia (Balibar, 2005; Fassin & Fassin, 2006; Ndiaye, 2008; Dorlin, 2009;

Bentouhami-Molino, 2015), analysts tend to follow a universalist and colour-blind Republican model. In this regard, until the 1990s, the strength of the Republican model pushed French public authorities to refuse any reference to racial discrimination. From their point of view, any mention of racial prejudices would implicitly give credit to the idea that races exist. However, the ban on the term "race" has not eliminated racism (Balibar, 2005; Fassin & Fassin, 2006; Bonilla Silva, 2014). Moreover, by absolutely rejecting the notion of race in the name of anti-racism, it becomes impossible to develop a profound reflection on the discriminations that are precisely based on it (Ndiaye, 2008). The controversy that emerged in February 2021, as the French Minister of Higher Education declared she would open an investigation on "Islamo-leftism in universities" that targeted scholars who referred to racialisation and intersectionality, underlines how sensitive these issues continue to be in French society.[2]

In Italy, scholars argue that after the second world war and the collapse of fascism, Italians tended to perceive themselves as being "innocent" in racist terms (Giuliani, 2015; Petrovich Njegosh & Scacchi, 2012). Racism was associated with the fascist regime, and racist terminology was removed from the scientific language. However, there was no process of deconstruction of the "figures of race" that had been central in the construction of the Italian national identity (Giuliani, 2015: 1). Although research on the racialisation of the labour market is emerging in Italy (Alberti & Iannuzzi, 2020; Piro & Sacchetto, 2021), scholars argue that there is a need to look at the "unconfessed realities" and challenge the illusion of Italian's "presumption of innocence" in racial themes (Faso, 2012).

While academics and institutions tend to be reluctant to analyse the essentialist processes that condition access to resources and jobs, essentialist and more specifically racialising discourses are far from being absent from the public debate. In France, since the middle of the 2000s, national debates, such as that on hijab-wearing, and those following the urban

[2] See, for instance, on the issue the press release by the French National Research Centre (CNRS) "Islamo-leftism" is not a scientific reality: https://www.cnrs.fr/en/islamo-leftism-not-scientific-reality-0

riots of 2005 and the 'terrorist attacks' of the 2010s, are saturated with racialised and often racist representations of the social world (Fassin & Fassin, 2006). In the same vein, scholars observe the trivialisation and legitimisation of the themes promoted by far-right parties such as the former *Front National*, particularly concerning migration, while media commentators have depoliticised the criticism towards these radical right parties (Maler & Salingue, 2014).

Similarly, in Italy, former *Lega Nord* gained media attention, especially from the 1990s precisely when the party started stigmatising migrants instead of targeting Southern Italians (Barcella, 2018). Since then, the party has grown exponentially, passing in a few years from two MPs in 1987 to over 180 MPs in 1994. Following the election of March 2018, the *Lega* obtained 124 seats in the Italian Chamber of Deputies, and its leader accessed the position of Ministry of Home Affairs for over a year. Meanwhile, essentialist and racist representations of migrants have proliferated in the Italian media during the last several decades (Ghebremariam Tesfau' & Picker, 2020), especially around the so-called "migrant crisis" (De Genova, 2018).

In the context of the polarisation of the political debate, it is more necessary than ever to study how essentialist processes condition access to resources and jobs. I argue that studying essentialism is crucial to understanding the stratifications of the labour market. These stratifications correspond to hierarchies among workers which result in differential salaries, working conditions, tasks, recognition, and all in all a differential of power and capabilities (Saunders, 1990; Yuval-Davis, 2015). Both in Italy (Fullin, 2016) and France (De Rudder & Vourc'h, 2006), researchers have highlighted that there are complex stratifications of the labour market based on gender, racialisation, nationality, status, age and other dimensions.

I propose to analyse stratifications and essentialism in the labour market by focusing on the specific challenges that migrant women with tertiary education face when accessing employment. In this regard, I argue that analysing the influence of essentialism in the recruitment and selection process permits us to comprehend why migrant women continue to be confined to jobs with low social recognition, despite their degrees. The perspective of migrant women with tertiary education[3] is particularly relevant to study the phenomena as they hold academic titles that should facilitate their access to positions in line with their studies (OECD, 2019). However, their migratory backgrounds, gender and essentialist representations of migrant women constitute cumulative disadvantages that prevent them from accessing the jobs they want (Purkayastha, 2005). Migrant women are particularly exposed to essentialist processes connected to the intersection of gender, migratory status, and country of birth, while they are also subject to different forms of racialisation (Scrinzi, 2013; Killian & Manohar, 2015).

Moreover, from a class perspective, these women tend to face contradictory class mobility when crossing borders (Parreñas, 2020), as they might simultaneously experience an increase in income and a decline in their professional status. The fact that many of these women used to be in positions of power in their country of birth and have experienced a loss or reduction of power in the country in which they migrate has led Riaño (2016) to qualify them as "marginalised elites". Lastly, the experience of these women is also of particular interest as, through their migration, they have navigated different migration and gender regimes and might have a transnational perspective on their experience (Kilkey & Merla, 2014).

The analysis of the book is based on multisited fieldwork. In this regard, scholars have argued that conducting research on similar groups of migrants in different places makes it possible to question generalisations based on single case studies and helps to further contextualise social phenomena (Bloemraad, 2013). Moreover, migration researchers have stressed the importance of locality in analysing migrants' experience (Schiller & Çağlar, 2009), while there have been also calls for studying employment mechanisms at the local level. For instance, Peck (1989) estimates that, although labour markets are constituted of wider structures, they are actually "constructed" at the local level. As a result, labour markets may be stratified in locally specific ways. Similarly, scholars have also argued that gender orders are local and that there are local patterns

---

[3] Tertiary education includes what is commonly understood as academic education but also advanced vocational or professional education (Unesco, 2012).

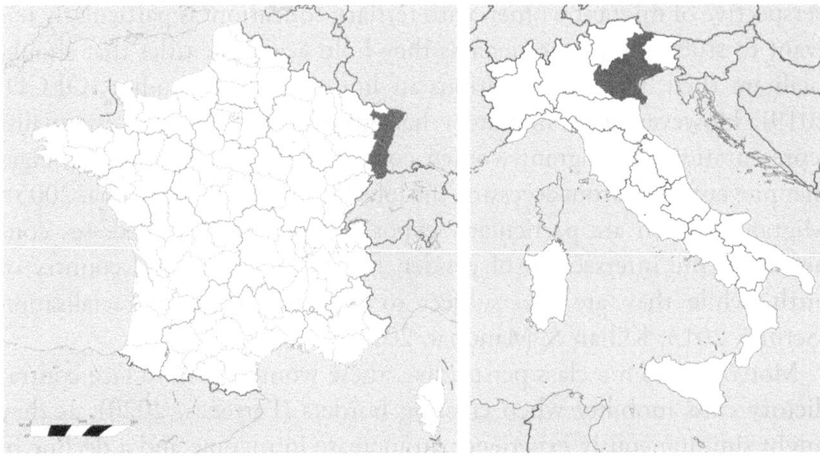

Map 1.1 Locating Alsace in France and Veneto in Italy. Credit: Niko67000, CC BY-SA 4.0, https://commons.wikimedia.org/w/index.php?curid=68972858 and TUBS - Italy location map.svg (by NordNordWest)., CC BY-SA 3.0, https://commons.wikimedia.org/w/index.php?curid=14512966

of gender relations (Jenkins, 2018). To take these observations into account, the study focuses on two local labour markets, namely those of Veneto in Italy, and Alsace in France (Map 1.1).

Veneto and Alsace share common features: if compared to the other regions of Italy and France, they are both characterised by a low level of unemployment (Istat, 2018a; Insee, 2021b) and a relatively high number of migrants in the entire population. In 2021, nearly 12% of inhabitants in Alsace were born abroad, while the same percentage of the Veneto population were foreigners (Insee, 2021a; Veneto Lavoro, 2022). Moreover, in both regions, migrants were mainly women. As far as access to the labour market is concerned, both regions show stratifications indicating that migrant women are more often concerned by unemployment and mainly access jobs with low social recognition compared to non-migrant women (Istat, 2018b; Insee, 2021c; Romens, 2019).

From a historical perspective, the two areas have different experiences of immigration. While 4% of the population was foreigners in Alsace already in the 1920s (Oriv, 2006), it reached that threshold in Veneto only by the end of the 1990s (Veneto Lavoro, 2022). However, in the first half of the twentieth century, both areas were embedded in national contexts regarded by colonialism. French and Italian colonial expansion went hand in hand with the whitening of the national identity and the hypersexualisation of racialised and colonised women (Dorlin, 2009; Petrovich Njegosh & Scacchi, 2012).

As far as migration *regimes*[4] are concerned, France and Italy tend to be classified into two different categories. France tends to be perceived as following a Republican model, in which the recognition of diversity is seen with suspicion (Fassin & Fassin, 2006). Conversely, scholars estimate that Italy follows a model of "subaltern integration" (Ambrosini, 2010), in which migrants are accepted only as long as they take the most humble jobs, without pretending to disrupt the social hierarchies or claiming working positions that the locals consider theirs. Moreover, it has been argued that the model that prevails in Northern Italy is that of "democratic differentiation", according to which migrants are perceived as holders of stable and homogeneous cultures that are ontologically different from the Italian one (Sacchetto, 2011). When it comes to comparing both contexts, Scrinzi (2013: 169) estimates that otherness is validated and censured in the context of French republican universalism, while it is idealised and stigmatised under Italian differentialism. We can wonder to which extent these different models influence the perception that stakeholders have of stratifications and essentialism in the labour market.

The analysis of the book is based on fieldwork that puts into dialogue the perspectives of different actors involved in the process of enabling migrant women with tertiary education to access employment, namely the women themselves, recruiters, and social workers. In this regard, scholars have argued that crossing subjects' perspectives provide distinct knowledge regarding the various aspects of a particular phenomenon. The idea is not that of achieving an "objective truth", but rather to grasp multiple subjective realities (Fauser, 2018).

When it comes to participants, my fieldwork included 51 narrative interviews (Flick, 2018): 28 of these were carried on in the Veneto region in Italy, while 23 focused on Alsace in France. Overall, thirty-three

[4] *Regimes* refer to clusters of state policies, cultures and practices, discourses, relations of power and inequalities, and forms of contestations (Bonizzoni, 2014).

migrant women with tertiary education participated in the research. The research participants had different working positions at the time of the interview. While most considered that their current job (or unemployment status) did not value their educational background, some were satisfied with their position. Nevertheless, they all referred to different forms of essentialism that have affected them or other migrant women and mentioned the strategies they had implemented to cope with essentialism and labour market stratifications.

To further provide a cross-section of views and perspectives, the research participants were born and had completed at least their secondary school in either a country of Sub-Saharan Africa or an Eastern European country outside of the EU.[5] Based on the literature (Grosfoguel et al., 2015), I hypothesised that women born in these two macro geographical areas could face different forms of racialisation in local labour markets. Moreover, scholars have called for further research on so-called *skilled* African women to challenge the dominant tropes that see these women as being uneducated, *immiserate*, and disempowered (Wong, 2014: 41).

Interviews were also conducted with 13 recruiters, both men and women, that worked in Alsace and Veneto. In this regard, scholars have stressed that access to employment by *skilled* migrant women has been little investigated from the perspective of labour market intermediaries (Ricci et al., 2021). Five of them worked for intermediary agencies that specialise in the selection of staff. Seven of them worked in the Human Resources department of private companies. Additionally, a member of the staff of the human resources department at an international organisation in France was also interviewed.

The interviews with migrant women and recruiters were complemented by those of four social workers; one of them worked for a public institution that aims at facilitating access to work, while three of them were employed in NGOs that supported migrants in accessing employment. In addition, my fieldwork also included the interview with an

[5] European non-EU countries of birth of participants were Albania, Armenia, Azerbaijan, Moldova, Russia, Turkey and Ukraine. Countries of birth from Sub-Saharan Africa were Cameroon, Congo, Democratic Republic of Congo, Mauritania, Niger, Nigeria, Senegal and South Africa.

NGO activist who has assisted migrants in the process of recognising titles gained abroad. Table 1.1 summarises the main characteristics of participants. To preserve their anonymity, their names were changed as well as the name of their employers, and other information that could make them recognisable.

Interviews were recorded and fully transcribed, except in one case in which the interviewee asked not to be audiotaped. The analysis of interviews mainly followed a thematic analysis (Terry et al., 2017). When analysing interviews, special attention was paid to the parts of narration in which interviewees referred to specific groups with which they were associated or that were external to them. Taking inspiration from critical discourse analysis (Fairclough, 2013), I took particular care in analysing these fragments, paying special attention to the vocabulary used to describe groups, in order to identify forms of essentialism. To facilitate the process of coding, the program *Maxqda* was used.

Before starting to interact with participants in my fieldwork, I was already familiar with several of the challenges that migrant women face when looking for a job. Indeed, my mother was herself a migrant woman with tertiary education who struggled to find employment in France. She was born in Colombia where she studied psychology and moved to France as a refugee at the beginning of the 1980s. As my mother received many negative answers when looking for a job in her field, she started working occasionally with refugees and migrants. After living over a decade in France, she decided to move back to Colombia where she felt it would be easier to get a job in her field.

To complete the considerations on my *positionality* (Burawoy, 2009) and my relation to the research topic, I would like to add a few words on my own trajectory. Indeed, critical scholars have emphasised that researchers do not live in a vacuum (Berger & Luckmann, 1991; Burawoy, 2009), but they are embedded in social relations in terms of class, gender, and racialisation, among others, that have an impact on the data they collect and the way they analyse social phenomena (Madge, 1992). As far as I am concerned, besides being the daughter of a migrant woman, I have also experienced migration myself. I was born in France and mainly lived between France and Colombia, before moving to Italy for family reasons. Therefore, some of my characteristics in the Italian context make me fit

Table 1.1 List of participants

Migrant women with tertiary education				
Alias	Born in	Education	Experience abroad	Experience in the area (Alsace/ Veneto)
Alsace (France)				
Callaia	Niger	Midwife school (Niger); nurse school (France)	Midwife	Nursing assistant in maternity; nurse
Abelia	Russia (Soviet Union)	Master's degree in pedagogy and littérature (Russia); Master's in slavic literature (France); degree librarian (France)		Shop assistant; librarian
Amapola	Albania	Master's in French literature (Albania)		Diplomat; bilingual administrative assistant
Colombine	South Africa	Bachelor's in theology (South Africa); Master's in English language and public exam CAPES (France)	Secretary; personal assistant	English tutor; English teacher
Amaryllis	Armenia (Soviet Union)	Bachelor's in pedagogy (Armenia); Master's in Slavic literature (France)	Teacher of Russian and English; translator	Flyer distributor; translator; cultural mediator; tutor
Araluen	Russia (Soviet Union)	Master's degree in literature (Russia); public competition CAPES (France)	Teacher of French language	Teacher of Russian language
Clemensia	Senegal	PhD in sociology (France)		Unemployed

(continued)

Table 1.1 (continued)

Migrant women with tertiary education				
Alias	Born in	Education	Experience abroad	Experience in the area (Alsace/ Veneto)
Carmel	Nigeria	Bachelor's in French language (Nigeria); Master's in human resources (France)	Bilingual secretary	English teacher; cleaner; hostess; grape picker; bilingual secretary; consultant; administrative assistant
Alexandra	Russia (Soviet Union)	Master's in literature (France); school for translation (France); PhD in Russian literature (San Marino)		Hostess; baby-sitter; translator; librarian; secretary; university professor
Azalea	Russia (Soviet Union)	Master's in economics (Russia)	Business manager	Flyer distributor; administrative assistant
Acacia	Moldova (Soviet Union)	Master's in Romanian and French literature (Moldova); Master's in education sciences (France)	Publisher; university lecturer; administrative civil servant	Tutor - private lessons; librarian; leader in a community Centre; receptionist
Acantha	Russia (Soviet Union)	Master's degree in economics (Russia); Master's in eco-counseling (France)	Commercial assistant, university lecturer	Translator; immovable consultant; local authority officer

(*continued*)

Table 1.1 (continued)

Migrant women with tertiary education				
Alias	Born in	Education	Experience abroad	Experience in the area (Alsace/ Veneto)
Camellia	Mauritania	Master's degree in sociology (Senegal); Master's in sociology (France); Master's in solidarity-based economy (France)	Consultant for NGOs	Waitress
Anemone	Azerbaijan (Soviet Union)	Master's in law and international relations (Azerbaijan)	Advisor to prosecutor	Maternity leave
Cliantha	Senegal	Bachelor's in sociology (Senegal); Bachelor's in sociology (France)	Waitress	Chambermaid
Aster	Ukraine (Soviet Union)	Phd in sociology (Germany)	Language teacher; project manager	Consultant for international organisations
Cassia	Senegal	Bachelor's management and IT (Senegal)	Salesperson; administrative assistant	Unemployed
Azami	Turkey	Master's degree in economics (Turkey)	Bank manager	Unemployed
Veneto (Italy)				
Rosella	Democratic Republic of Congo	Master's in medicine (Italy); public competition for physicians (Italy)		Domestic worker; baby-sitter; physician

(*continued*)

Table 1.1 (continued)

Migrant women with tertiary education				
Alias	Born in	Education	Experience abroad	Experience in the area (Alsace/ Veneto)
Winika	Ukraine (Soviet Union)	Bachelor's in music teaching (Ukraine)	Music teacher; accountant	In-home carer; waitress; pizza maker
Zinnia	Albania	Bachelor's in foreign languages (Italy)		Hostess; check-in assistant; call-Centre; call-Centre; sales assistant;
Rosalie	Democratic Republic of Congo	Diploma in laboratory technics (DRC); vocational training as care assistant (Italy)	Laboratory assistant	Blue-collar; care assistant
Violet	Russia (Soviet Union)	Bachelor's in German/English languages (Russia); training as a sommelier and sales manager (Italy)	Language teacher, business assistant in corporations	Business assistant; export manager
Yasmin	Ukraine (Soviet Union)	Bachelor's in forestry and international relations (Ukraine); Bachelor's in foreign languages and cultures (Italy)	Assistant to professors; translator	Cultural mediator; translator; tutor for professional training; hostess; business manager
Veronica	Ukraine (Soviet Union)	Master's in business (Ukraine); PhD in economy and management (Italy)	Administrative assistant	English teacher; translator; project manager; business manager; coach (gym)

(continued)

Table 1.1 (continued)

Migrant women with tertiary education				
Alias	Born in	Education	Experience abroad	Experience in the area (Alsace/Veneto)
Rosamel	Cameroon	Bachelor's in physiotherapy (Italy); diploma in osteopathy (Italy)		Physiotherapist
Rose	Congo	Bachelor's in communication sciences (Italy)	Salesperson	Cleaning operative; university caretaker; cook assistant
Rada	Cameroon	Bachelor's in tri-lingual literature (Cameroon); Master's in political sciences and human rights (Italy)		Cleaning operative; cultural mediator; social support assistant
Rosanna	Cameroon	Bachelor's in economics (Italy); vocational training as care assistant (Italy)		Shelf-stacker; cleaning operative; inventory assistant; in-home carer; care assistant
Varda	Albania	Bachelor's in statistics (Italy)		Ice-cream parlour; waitress
Raisa	Cameroon	Master's in economics (Cameroon); Master's in communication sciences and marketing (Italy)		Cultural mediator

(*continued*)

Table 1.1 (continued)

Migrant women with tertiary education				
Alias	Born in	Education	Experience abroad	Experience in the area (Alsace/ Veneto)
Viola	Russia (Soviet Union)	Master's in English philology (Russia); diploma of Russian as a foreign language (Russia)	Tutor; translator; financial officer; editor; university lecturer	Russian teacher in private schools
Verbena	Albania	Bachelor's in Albanian language and literature and Master's in humanities (Albania)	Teacher	Maternity leave
Labour market gatekeepers				
Name	**Position**		**Experience in**	**Gender**
Dalia	Recruiter in an HR department		Alsace	Woman
Drake	Recruiter in an intermediary agency		Alsace	Man
Elm	Recruiter in an HR department		Alsace	Man
Saffron	Recruiter in an intermediary agency		Veneto	Man
Senecio	Previously: Recruiter in an intermediary agency		Veneto	Man
Senna	Recruiter in an HR department		Veneto	Woman
Sequoia	Recruiter in an HR department		Veneto	Man
Shamrock	Recruiter in an HR department		Veneto	Man
Sirelli	Previously: Recruiter in an intermediary agency/now: Recruiter in an HR department		Veneto	Woman
Sorrel	Recruiter in an intermediary agency		Veneto	Man
Susan	Recruiter in an HR department		Veneto	Woman
Suzette	Recruiter in an HR department		Veneto	Woman

(continued)

Table 1.1 (continued)

Migrant women with tertiary education				
Alias	Born in	Education	Experience abroad	Experience in the area (Alsace/ Veneto)
Sycamore	Recruiter in an HR department		Veneto	Man
Daphne	Social worker		Alsace	Woman
Dianella	Social worker		Alsace	Woman
Salma	Social worker		Veneto	Woman
Selena	Social worker		Veneto	Woman
Marc	NGO activist		Veneto	Man

into the social group that I intended to study. My gender, my level of education, and my otherness as a migrant are commonalities. However, as I hold a French passport, the administrative challenges I had to face when moving to Italy were far more straightforward than those of my interviewees. Besides, the way I am racialised in both contexts also differs from my participants and might vary depending on whether I am perceived as a Colombian or as a French, and therefore as a citizen of two countries that have different positions in the international arena, contrasting colonial histories, and whose nationals are being essentialised differently. Overall, the way I was perceived by participants in my fieldwork might have facilitated, to a certain extent, the building of relationships of trust with migrant women interviewees, while it might have reinforced the *impression management* of recruiters, namely their attempt to control their answers to make a positive impression on me (Hester & Francis, 1994).

When it comes to the structure of the book, the publication is divided into six chapters. After the **first introductory chapter**, the **second chapter** presents the lenses through which the challenges that migrant women face in accessing employment are analysed. It also reviews the literature and identifies gaps. It is precisely based on these omissions that the research questions are elaborated on at the end of the chapter. The **third chapter** aims at studying the stratifications of the local labour markets, and how essentialism influences access to employment, by crossing the perspectives of migrant women with tertiary education, recruiters and social workers. The **fourth chapter** studies the mechanisms that lie behind stratifications, emphasising the role of essentialism in the recruitment and selection process. More specifically, it analyses how knowledge, know-how, capacities, and skills are embodied and assessed depending on who holds them. It studies how essentialism based on racialisation, gender and class influences recruiters' assessment of education, experience, as well as language and soft skills. The **fifth chapter** stresses the *agency* of migrant women with tertiary education, by studying how these women are coping, resisting, and eventually challenging essentialism. It also analyses the strategies that migrant women implement to access employment and eventually cope with downgrading. The book ends with the **sixth chapter** which highlights its contribution to the literature and provides insights for future research.

By analysing the challenges faced by migrant women with tertiary education, the book highlights how access to resources and employment is gendered, classed, and racialised and how essentialist processes influence it. Understanding the mechanisms that contribute to reproducing stratifications aids in designing paths toward more equal access to employment.

References

Alberti, G., & Iannuzzi, F. E. (2020). Embodied intersectionality and the intersectional management of hotel labour: The everyday experiences of social differentiation in customer-oriented work. *Gender, Work and Organization, 27*(6), 1165–1180.

Ambrosini, M. (2010). Giovani di origine immigrata: costruzioni identitarie e processi di integrazione. In M. V. Calvi, G. Mapelli, & M. Bonomi (Eds.), *Lingua, identità e immigrazione* (pp. 23–35). FrancoAngeli.

Balibar, É. (2005). La construction du racisme. *Actuel Marx, 2*, 11–28.

Barcella, P. (2018). Percorsi leghisti: dall'antimeridionalismo alla xenofobia. *Meridian, 91*, 95–119.

Bentouhami-Molino, H. (2015). *Race, cultures, identités. Une approche féministe et postcoloniale*. Puf.

Berger, P. L., & Luckmann, T. (1991). *The social construction of reality*. Penguin books.

Bloemraad, I. (2013). The promise and pitfalls of comparative research design in the study of migration. *Migration studies, 1*(1), 27–46.
Bonilla Silva, E. (2014). *Racism without racists*. Rowman & Littlefield.
Bonizzoni, P. (2014). Immigrant working mothers reconciling work and childcare: The experience of Latin American and Eastern European women in Milan. *Social Politics: International Studies in Gender State & Society, 21*(2) 194–217. https://doi.org/10.1093/sp/jxu008
Brandi, M. C. (2010). Le migrazioni qualificate dall'Europa dell'Est verso l'Italia. *Studi Emigrazione, XLVII*, 179.
Burawoy, M. (2009). *The extended case method*. University of California Press.
Chiswick, B. R., & Miller, P. W. (2009). The international transferability of immigrants' human capital. *Economics of Education Review, 28*(2), 162–169.
Coccia, B., & Pittau, F. (Eds.). (2016). *Le migrazione qualificate in Italia. Ricerche, statistiche, prospettive*. Centro Studi e Ricerche IDOS.
De Genova, N. (2018). The "migrant crisis" as racial crisis: Do black lives matter in Europe? *Ethnic and Racial Studies, 41*(10), 1765–1782.
De Rudder, V., & Vourc'h, F. (2006). Les discriminations racistes dans le monde du travail. In D. Fassin & E. Fassin (Eds.), *De la question sociale à la question raciale ? Représenter la société française*. La Découverte.
Dorlin, E. (2009). *La matrice de la race. Généalogie sexuelle et coloniale de la Nation française*. La Découverte.
Fairclough, N. (2013). *Critical discourse analysis: The critical study of language*. Routledge.
Faso, G. (2012). Prefazione. In T. Petrovich Njegosh & A. Scacchi (Eds.), *Parlare di razza. La lingua del colore tra Italia e Stati Uniti*. Ombre corte.
Fassin, D., & Fassin, E. (2006). *De la question sociale à la question raciale ? Représenter la société française*. La Découverte.
Fauser, M. (2018). Mixed methods and multisited migration research: Innovations from a transnational perspective. *Journal of Mixed Methods Research, 12*(4), 394–412.
Flick, U. (2018). *An introduction to qualitative research*. Sage.
Fullin, G. (2016). Labour market outcomes of immigrants in a south European country: Do race and religion matter? *Work, Employment and Society, 30*(3), 391–409.
Ghebremariam Tesfau', M., & Picker, G. (2020). The Italian postracial archive. *Ethnic and Racial Studies, 44*(2), 195–214.
Giuliani, G. (Ed.). (2015). *Il colore della nazione*. Le Monnier università.

Grigoleit-Richter, G. (2017). Highly skilled and highly mobile? Examining gendered and ethnicised labour market conditions for migrant women in STEM-professions in Germany. *Journal of Ethnic and Migration Studies, 43*(16), 2738–2755.

Grosfoguel, R., Oso, L., & Christou, A. (2015). 'Racism', intersectionality and migration studies: Framing some theoretical reflections. *Identities, 22*(6), 635–652.

Grosz, E. (1990). A note on essentialism and difference. In S. Gunew (Ed.), *Feminist knowledge: Critique and construct* (pp. 332–344). Routledge.

Hester, S., & Francis, D. (1994). Doing data: The local organization of a sociological interview. *British Journal of Sociology, 45*, 675–695.

Insee. (2021a). *Population immigrée selon le sexe et l'âge en 2018, database.* Available at: https://www.insee.fr/fr/statistiques/2012730

Insee. (2021b). *Taux de chômage localisés par sexe et âge en moyenne annuelle en 2020.* Available at https://www.insee.fr/fr/statistiques/2134411

Insee. (2021c). *IMG2A V2 - Population de 15 ans ou plus par sexe, âge, situation quant à l'immigration et type d'activité en 2018Recensement de la population.* Available at: https://www.insee.fr/fr/statistiques/5397755

Istat. (2018a). *Tasso di disoccupazione - livello regionale. Rilevazione della forza lavoro.* disponibile dal sito: http://dati.istat.it/

Istat. (2018b). *Popolazione per condizione professionale. Rilevazione della forza lavoro.* disponibile dal sito: http://dati.istat.it/

Jenkins, S. (2018). *Gender, place and the labour market.* Routledge.

Kilkey, M., & Merla, L. (2014). Situating transnational families' care-giving arrangements: The role of institutional contexts. *Global Networks, 14*(2), 210–229.

Killian, C., & Manohar, N. N. (2015). Highly skilled immigrant Women's labor market access. *Social Currents, 3*(2), 138–159.

Kofman, E. (2012). Gender and skilled migration in Europe. *Cuadernos de Relaciones Laborales, 30*(1), 63–89.

Lentin, A. (2014). Postracial silences: The othering of race in Europe. In W. D. Hund & A. Lentin (Eds.), *Racism and sociology*. Lit Verlag.

Liversage, A. (2009). Vital conjunctures, shifting horizons: High-skilled female immigrants looking for work, *work. Employment & Society, 23*(1), 120–141.

Madge, C. (1992). Boundary disputes: Comments on Sidaway. *Area, 25*(3), 294–299.

Maler, H., & Salingue, J. (2014). Front national: Indignations sélectives et banalisation effective. *Savoir/Agir, 29*(3), 95–103.

Mukasonga Scholastique. (2018). *Un si beau diplôme!* Gallimard.
Ndiaye, P. (2008). *La condition noire. Essai sur une minorité française.* Calmann-Lévy.
OECD. (2014). *Perspectives des migrations internationales 2014.* OECD Publishing.
OECD. (2019). *Education at a glance 2019: OECD indicators.* OECD Publishing.
ORIV. (2006). *"Étrangers et immigrés en Alsace" – Guide pour comprendre et agir.* Available at: http://www.oriv.org/documents/etrangers-et-immigres-en-alsace-guide-pour-comprendre-et-agir/
Parreñas, R. (2020). *Servants of globalization: Migration and domestic work.* Stanford University Press.
Peck, J. A. (1989). Reconceptualizing the local labour market: Space, segmentation and the state. *Progress in Human Geography, 13*(1), 42–61.
Petrovich Njegosh, T., & Scacchi, A. (2012). *Parlare di razza. La lingua del colore tra Italia e Stati Uniti.* Ombre corte.
Piro, V., & Sacchetto, D. (2021). Subcontracted racial capitalism: The interrelationship of race and production in meat processing plants. *Work in the Global Economy, 1*(1–2), 33–53.
Purkayastha, B. (2005). Skilled migration and cumulative disadvantage: The case of highly qualified Asian Indian immigrant women in the US. *Geoforum, 36*, 181–196. https://doi.org/10.1016/j.geoforum.2003.11.006
Purkayastha, D., & Bircan, T. (2021). Present but not counted: Highly skilled migrant women in Belgium. *Journal of Ethnic and Migration Studies, 43*(13), 1–19.
Riaño, Y. (2016). Minga biographic workshops with highly skilled migrant women: Enhancing spaces of inclusion. *Qualitative Research, 16*(3), 267–279.
Ricci, A., Crivellaro, F., & Bolzani, D. (2021). Perceived employability of highly skilled migrant women in STEM: Insights from labor market intermediaries' professionals. *Administrative Sciences, 11*(1), 7.
Romens, A.-I. (2019). Accesso a un mercato del lavoro segmentato: laureate migranti in Veneto. *Mondi Migranti, 39*(3), 153–180.
Sacchetto, D. (2011). *Xenophobia or democratic differentiation? A new path of separation and discipline for migrant workers in Italy. Contemporary centrifugal regionalism: Comparing Flanders and Northern Italy* (pp. 141–155). Kvab.
Saunders, P. (1990). *Social class and stratification.* Routledge.

Schiller, N. G., & Çağlar, A. (2009). Towards a comparative theory of locality in migration studies: Migrant incorporation and city scale. *Journal of Ethnic and Migration Studies, 35*(2), 177–202.

Scrinzi, F. (2013). *Genre, migrations et emplois domestiques en France et en Italie. Construction de la non-qualification et de l'altérité ethnique*. Pétra.

Terry, G., Hayfield, N., Clarke, V., & Braun, V. (2017). Thematic analysis. In C. Willig & W. S. Rogers (Eds.), *The SAGE handbook of qualitative research in psychology* (pp. 17–37). SAGE.

Tognetti Bordogna, M. (2012). *Donne e percorsi migratori*. Franco Angeli.

UNESCO. (2012). *International standard classification of education*. UNESCO Institute for Statistics.

Veneto Lavoro. (2022). *Veneto: dinamica della popolazione residente, data-base*. Available at: http://www.venetolavoro.it/popolazione-residente

Wong, M. (2014). Geographies and strategies of caregiving among skilled Ghanaian migrant women. *Women's Studies International Forum, 42*(1), 28–43.

Yuval-Davis, N. (2015). Situated intersectionality and social inequality. *Raisons Politiques, 58*(2), 91–100.

2

"I Became a Migrant from Eastern Europe". Essentialism and Migrant Women with Tertiary Education

When I first met Viola in Veneto, she was struggling to find a way to get employment in line with her studies. Viola graduated in Philology and had a rewarding position in Russia where she used to work as a lecturer for a prestigious State University and as a financial director for a well-known museum. After over a decade of being active in the labour market, she started to feel bored. Although Viola was still finding that her jobs were interesting, she wanted to experience new professional challenges and start a family at the same time. As a result, she decided to quit her jobs, abandon her social position, and join her partner with whom she had become acquainted a couple of years before. The result was a move to Veneto where her partner lived. During our exchange, Viola contrasted the respected position she had in Russia with the denigration she was facing in Veneto. She explained that she felt labelled and categorised as "a migrant from Eastern Europe" and as such, she felt devalued and disrespected.

Since the 1960s, the practice and consequences of labelling, categorising, and eventually discrediting others' capacities, have been the subject of a consistent body of literature in sociology (Goffman, 1990) as well as in social psychology (Moscovici, 2015). Sociologists have highlighted the

A.-I. Romens, *Deconstructing Essentialism*,
https://doi.org/10.1007/978-3-031-14399-1_2

political implications of using specific categories to refer to groups of people. In this regard, Bourdieu (1993) estimates that one of the central powers of the State is to produce mental structures, or categories of thought, which predetermine and organise our representation of the world. From Sayad's perspective (2016), the notion of "immigrant" is one of these mental structures. Nevertheless, categories and concepts are needed to analyse social phenomena. Therefore, when conducting research, it is necessary to have a critical awareness of the political implications of using a specific wording and conceptual framework.

To take into account these observations, the chapter defines terms and introduces the theoretical lens that is used to study the access that migrant women with tertiary education have to local labour markets. It also reviews the literature on the issue through the prism of essentialism and pays specific attention to racialisation, gender and class relations. The exercise makes it possible to identify gaps in the literature and define the research questions that are listed in the conclusions of the chapter.

2.1 Who the Skilled Are

Scholars have argued that *skilled* migration has become the most "acceptable" form of migration, especially when entering high-income countries with 'points-based schemes' (Boucher, 2020). In this regard, the notion of skills works as a social marker that creates a symbolic boundary between desirable *skilled* and undesirable *unskilled* migrants (Vasey, 2021). However, although the concept of skilled migration is frequently used within policies and in academic research, there is no shared definition of what it covers and skills remain a highly contested domain (Mezzadra & Neilson, 2013). Indeed, within policy design and in scholarly debate, the varying definitions of skills have significant consequences regarding whose migrants are to be accepted and regarded as skilled, in terms of gender, class and racialisation.

Within policies, skills tend to be defined according to a complex and varying combination of criteria that include a wage threshold, occupying highly qualified employment, holding tertiary education, and language proficiency (Boucher, 2020). For instance, Coccia and Pittau (2016) note that migrants are often considered as being "highly skilled" when they hold a tertiary education qualification, but the concept might also refer to persons that engage in a profession that is considered at the top of the employment structure such as managers and top professionals in the health, banking, and academic sectors. A third way of defining the concepts regards income. This is the case within the 2009 EU directive (European Council, 2009) which promotes the *Blue Card* residence permit system. The latter aims at regulating the access of non-EU citizens to "highly qualified" jobs in the EU Member States, which are defined according to a salary threshold. To obtain this residence permit, candidates must prove they have a gross annual salary equivalent to a minimum salary threshold which "shall be at least 1,5 times the average gross annual salary in the Member State concerned".

Defining *skilled migrants* based on income or on whether they hold a top-job position has major implications in terms of gender, class and racialisation. From a gender perspective, women tend to earn less than men and have more difficulties in accessing top-management positions (Arulampalam et al., 2007). As a result, migration schemes such as the *Blue Card* system tend to privilege men over women (Kofman, 2012). From a class perspective, Coccia and Pittau (2016) argue that definitions based on income exclusively encompass "top earners" and ignore "intellectuals" and "graduates". Indeed, economic capital is the main focus and other forms of capital, such as cultural capital, are underestimated by these definitions. As far as racialisation is concerned, in post-colonial societies (Bonilla Silva, 2014) and segmented labour markets (Castles & Miller, 2009), those racialised as whites have privileged working positions compared to those racialised as non-whites. As a result, the term skilled migrants might predominantly refer to white men from top-income groups of the Global North.

To address these critics, rather than referring to *skilled* migration, the book uses the less misleading notion of tertiary education, which builds on secondary education and includes what is commonly understood as academic education but also advanced vocational or professional education (Unesco, 2012). The book focuses on the experience of migrant women that have obtained a degree or certificate from academic institutions or advanced vocational training, regardless of the country where it was acquired.

2.2 The Literature on Migrant Women with Tertiary Education

Although there has been a growing number of publications that have focused on the issue, scholars stress that there is still a need to further *engender* research on migrants with tertiary education (Triandafyllidou & Isaakyan, 2016). Feminist scholars have pointed out that the notion of gender in migration studies is often equated to that of studying women, rather than analysing the power relations between women and men and the social construction around femininities and masculinities (Fresnoza-Flot & Shinozaki, 2017). Engendering migration studies involves acknowledging that gender relations are a "constitutive element" of migration: they structure migration, and mobility transforms gender relations (Hondagneu-Sotelo, 2003).

The literature that concerns migrant women with tertiary education has covered a range of sectors and issues, paying special attention to their experience in jobs involving social reproduction, from in-home care assistants to nurses (Yeates, 2009; Cuban, 2013; Likupe, 2015). In this regard, Raghuram (2008) argued that research tended to focus on feminised reproductive sectors while little had been written on migrant women with tertiary education in male-dominated areas. Meanwhile, recent publications have analysed the experience of these women in ICTs (Gropas & Bartolini, 2016), medicine (Wojczewski et al., 2015), academia (Shinozaki, 2017), business (Grigoleit, 2010), and Science, Technology, Engineering, and Maths (Grigoleit-Richter, 2017; Ricci et al., 2021; Bolzani et al., 2021).

One of the main issues explored by this literature regards the *contradictory class mobility* (Parreñas, 2020) experienced by migrant women when entering the labour markets of the Global North (Cuban, 2013; Wojczewski et al., 2015). The concept refers to the fact that migrant women can simultaneously experience upward mobility, connected to their increasing income, and downward mobility related to the decline of their professional and social status. In this regard, researchers have stressed that migrant women, and more specifically those racialised from the Global South (Wong, 2014), tend to access positions at the bottom of the employment structure, especially in the care sector, and end up being *deskilled* (Cuban, 2013; Kofman, 2012). Researchers have also highlighted that the trajectories of migrant women with tertiary education are highly dependent on the gender order that prevails in the country of immigration (Riaño, 2012; Purkayastha & Bircan, 2021). Recent publications have also analysed the obstacles these women face when accessing employment from an intersectional perspective (Rodriguez & Scurry, 2019; Bolzani et al., 2021). However, none of these studies has especially focused on the way essentialism shapes their labour opportunities. Section 2.3 will further analyse the factors identified by the literature to explain why migrant women, including those with tertiary education, tend to be confined to jobs with low social recognition.

When it comes to studies that focus on France, scholars point out that the research on the employment positioning of migrant women mainly focuses on access to social reproductive jobs, which feeds the stereotype that associates them with domestic and care work (Dumitru, 2019). Nevertheless, over the last decade, some publications have also studied the trajectories of migrant women with tertiary education in other sectors, stressing that they are particularly exposed to contradictory class mobility (Cossée et al., 2012; Sirna, 2020; Jentjens, 2021), especially if they were born in countries of the former colonial empire (Killian & Manohar, 2015). In Italy, the limited literature that analyses the trajectories of migrants with tertiary education (Brandi, 2010; Bussola & Pelliccia, 2012; Coccia & Pittau, 2016), rarely focuses on women (Bolzani et al., 2021). Until recently, the experience of migrant women with tertiary education was mainly analysed tangentially within broader research that focused on migrant women in general (Vianello, 2009; Toffanin, 2015). Therefore, this book intends to study the experience of migrant women with tertiary education in two countries where their trajectories have been little explored.

2.3 A Conditioned Access to Stratified Labour Markets

Researchers have developed different theories to explain why migrant women with tertiary education tend to experience contradictory class mobility when migrating (Parreñas, 2020). The following paragraphs review this literature and introduce explanatory factors at the macro-, meso- and micro-level, stressing the gaps in the literature.

Labour Demand in the Global North Various theoretical approaches have tried to explain the inequalities between migrants and non-migrants that access the labour market. Macro-structural theories focus on the demand for labour: migrants would be forced to accept low-paid positions that the natives refuse. Castles and Miller (2009: 222) highlight that the need for "low-skilled labour" in economies of the Global North is socially constructed and based on poor wages, conditions and status in some sectors, which leads natives to avoid certain types of jobs. Rather than a need for migrant labour, Castles and Miller argue that it is the demand that is put forward by "powerful economic and political interests". Through migration policies and new employment forms characterised by subcontracting, temporary work and casualisation, migrants continue to be transformed into a "subordinate, flexible labour force" (Castles & Miller, 2009: 234). Tsing (2009) argues that "difference" has a structural role in the mobilisation of capital, labour and resources. She especially analyses how economic, cultural and gender diversity plays a constitutive role in supply chain capitalism. It enables employers to cut labour costs and dictate (self)exploiting working conditions without endorsing any responsibility. Through the case of migrant women with tertiary education, the book further develops the argument of Tsing (2009) and illustrates how difference is perceived and used by employers as an asset to increase profits.

Migration Regimes Scholars have highlighted the multiple implications that migratory policies have in confining migrants at the bottom of the employment structure. For instance, as migrants' administrative status might rely on having an employment contract, they might look for any job as long as it enables them to access a residence permit (Morris, 2001). Consequently, migrants would more readily accept positions at the bottom of the employment market, which are unstable and poorly paid. As a result, they are particularly exposed to exploitation at work (Terray, 2008). When it comes to policies on skilled migration, we mentioned that they are selective in terms of gender, racialisation and class.

Moreover, feminist researchers have pointed out that family reunification policies are guided by gender-stereotyped ideas (Riaño, 2012; Purkayastha & Bircan, 2021). For instance, women with tertiary education do not enter countries of destination only as workers but also as students, refugees and with other statuses. Many of them reunite in the context of family migration. However, family residence permits might provide only limited access to the labour market preventing these women from achieving their aspirations. An additional barrier regards access to positions in the public sector, as they might be closed to foreigners (Kofman, 2012; Daadouch, 2007), whereas in the private sector regulations might give priority to national or European workers (Riaño, 2012). For instance, the so-called *Guéant circular*, adopted in France in 2011 and which was mentioned by participants in my fieldwork, indicated that employers wanting to hire a non-EU citizen had to prove they did not find a French or an EU candidate for the position. Although the text was revoked a few years later, norms continue to discourage the recruitment and selection of non-EU citizens, as employers still need to pay a specific tax and have additional paperwork to fill in to hire a non-EU candidate.

Networks and Labour Market Positioning The literature has highlighted the centrality of networks in defining the migration project and work placement (Portes & Bach, 1985). Informal networks and social capital provide vital resources and cultural capital to individuals in their migratory process (Castles & Miller, 2009). As a result, Tognetti Bordogna (2012) emphasises that skills and aspirations often become secondary while belonging to a specific nationality comes first. Indeed, in labour markets that are highly stratified on the base of gender, migratory status and citizenship, the use of national networks can limit access to positions at the bottom of the employment structure. For instance, migrant women with tertiary education might more easily find work in the same employment sector than their co-national friends. If the latter all work as care workers, newcomers might have access to the same position, despite their level of education. As a result, the stratifications of the labour market tend to self-reproduce: Unless they can count on social capital outside of their national group, migrants access jobs depending on their nationality. In France, Killian and Manohar (2015) observe that colonialism has placed formerly colonised subjects at the bottom of the employment structure. As a consequence, women with tertiary education who migrate from the former colonial space might primarily count on a network which has little access to middle and top positions. Their social capital might limit their employment opportunities, providing only access to positions at the bottom of the employment structure and to "ethnic economies" that offer small compensation to their human capital (Zhou & Logan, 1998). Although it is not the main focus, this book takes into account the social capital of the research participants and the way it has influenced their trajectories.

Mothering, Welfare and Care Regime Although women in Western Europe have increasingly been participating in the labour market, gender ideologies continue to convey the idea that mothers should be the main carers of their children. Women remain the primary providers of unpaid reproductive work (Kofman & Raghuram, 2015), leading to what Balbo (1978) has called the double presence (*doppia presenza*), meaning that they are involved in both productive (or reproductive) work in the labour market, and unpaid reproductive work at home. In this context, access to care provision is key to enabling migrant women to have a career, and regimes that retain the locus of care within the family might reinforce the conventional gendered division of labour (Shinozaki, 2014). A consistent body of literature has studied the interconnection between care and migration regimes, focusing on the presence of migrant women working in the domestic and care sectors. For instance, scholars have theorised concepts such as that of *global care chains* or *circuits of care*, to emphasise how women from the Global South are migrating to care for children of women from the Global North, leaving their children behind and supporting them at a distance (Williams, 2010; Parreñas, 2020). With these theories, scholars highlight the irony of women from the Global North getting broader access to the labour market at the expense of women from the Global South (Williams, 2010). However, this is not the only way in which care and migration intersect and shape migrant women's trajectories. Scholars have stressed that mothering status is crucial to understanding the professional trajectories of migrant women with tertiary education, although the issue has been understudied in the literature (Wong, 2014; Shinozaki, 2017; Romens, 2021). The intersection between care and migration regimes might be critical in enabling migrant women to access care services and be able to work. When the public childcare system is not accessible or underdeveloped, migrant women have to rely on the combination of formal and informal resources to care for their children and be able to work. Partners as well as the network of family members, friends, neighbours, or co-nationals can become crucial to combine work and care for children. Although relevant to understanding migrant women's position in the labour market, the book will not focus on this aspect.

The Lack of Recognition of Skills Part of the literature on migration has focused on the "less-than-perfect international transferability" of skills (Chiswick & Miller, 2009). Different theories have been developed to explain the "educational mismatch" between occupation and over-education. For instance, the *search and match theory* argues that the mismatch is related to imperfect information in the labour market that mainly affects those entering the labour market for the first time (Groot & Van Den Maassen, 2000). Another example is that of the *human capital theory*, which underlines that migrants have difficulties in transferring both formal schooling and labour market experience across borders (Chiswick & Miller, 2009). According to this theory, labour market entrants may take jobs that require less education with the intention of gaining experience. Scholars have stressed that this literature overlooks the role of labour market gatekeepers in reproducing labour market stratifications (Almeida & Fernando, 2017). To provide a more detailed analysis of these mechanisms, recent publications have focused on how organisation- and occupation-specific factors influence decision-makers in the recruitment and selection of migrant candidates (Ibid). In line with the *social identity theory* (Tajfel & Turner, 1986), these studies highlight that recruiters, especially local recruiters who are unfamiliar with other cultural backgrounds, tend to opt for in-group candidates, excluding migrants from the selection process regardless of their academic and professional backgrounds. All these theories claim that over-education declines with duration. However, the literature on migrant women with tertiary education has emphasised that deskilling is a lasting process and that, as time passes, it might even become more difficult for migrant women to access their previous field of work (Cuban, 2013). Another critical limit of this literature is that it does not take into account essentialism nor gender, racialisation, and class.

2.4 Focusing on Essentialism

To address the gap in the literature, the book proposes to analyse the underlying mechanisms that lead to the stratification of the labour market, by focusing on the impact that essentialism has in the recruitment and selection of staff. More specifically, it studies how recruiters' and other labour market gatekeepers' essentialist representations influence the assessment of skills, leading to the devaluation of migrant women's capacities.

Defining Essentialism In the book, essentialism is defined as a process through which people become defined as a group based on alleged biological or cultural characteristics. I refer to Grosz (1990)'s definition of essentialism:

> *Essentialism [...] refers to the attribution of a fixed essence to women, [which] is assumed to be given, universal, and is usually, though not necessarily, identified with women's biology and "natural "characteristics. [...] Essentialism entails that those characteristics defined as women's essence are shared in common by all women at all times. [...] Essentialism thus refers to the existence of fixed characteristics, given attributes, and ahistorical functions which limit the possibilities of change and thus of social reorganisation.* (Grosz, 1990: 334)

Although Grosz focuses on women, her definition highlights features that encompass forms of essentialism based on racialisation, the reification of cultural differences, and that associate specific traits and attitudes with specific nationalities. Indeed, racialisation can be approached as a form of essentialism, that uses markers such as the colour of the skin, the country of birth, culture or religion to justify superiority and privilege (Grosfoguel et al., 2015). It occurs through the marking of bodies: some are racialised as superior, others as inferior. As such, race is a social construct that was historically and politically created, recreated and challenged (Ndiaye, 2008; Petrovich Njegosh & Scacchi, 2012) and served as a scientific argument to justify material and symbolic domination (Bonilla Silva, 2014; Ndiaye, 2008; Fassin & Fassin, 2006). For instance, racialisation was instrumental to the development and perpetuation of the slave trade, the eradication of native peoples, and the expansion of white

Europeans who perceived themselves as empowered "via divine guidance and endorsement" to civilise the world (Quraishi & Philburn, 2015).

For post- and de-colonial researchers, the divide inherited from colonialism is still a matter of fact. Grosfoguel et al. (2015) stress that global hierarchies of power put in place by Western colonial administrations did not disappear with the end of colonial administration. The racism that emerged with colonialism continues to thrive. Adopting a decolonial approach is of particular relevance for analysing how migrants are being racialised in European societies. In this regard, Grosfoguel et al. (2015) stress that migrants who move to Europe do not arrive in neutral spaces, but in spaces that are already 'polluted' by racial power relations inherited from coloniality. Based on the colonial past (but not only) migrants are racialised in European societies depending on markers such as the colour of their skin, their country of birth, their culture or their religion, but also according to gender, class, and other social relations that intersect.

Focusing on the concept of essentialism enables us to adopt an intersectional approach (Crenshaw, 1989; Browne & Misra, 2003) that permits us to highlight how racialisation interacts with other forms of essentialism based on gender, and class. Broadening Grosz's definition, we can argue that essentialism entails that those externally defined as a group, in terms of gender, class, and racialisation, all share presumed "essential" characteristics. From the perspective of those who essentialise, the alleged characteristics are fixed, ahistorical, and cannot be changed since they define and limit the group, which limits the possibilities of social reorganisation. Essentialism is imposed by a dominant group on an oppressed group, to justify inequality in access to resources, including to graduate jobs.

I propose to analyse, identify and deconstruct essentialist discourses and practices in the recruitment and selection of staff, by focusing on essentialism based on the intersection of racialisation, gender and class. Although other social relations, such as religion, sexual orientation, age, and disability, among others, have a significant impact in facilitating or preventing access to employment, they are not explored here in detail.

Essentialism in the Recruitment and Selection Process The book studies how essentialism impacts migrant women's access to jobs and influences the recruitment and selection of staff. *Recruitment* corresponds to tasks such as job analysis, description, ads, person specification and competency framework and *selection* to interviews and short-listing (Almeida & Fernando, 2017). Scholars have argued that gender, racial and class ideologies are crucial in naturalising capacities into specific bodies, hiding the efforts that workers put into performing specific tasks (Wolkowitz, 2006). For instance, gender ideology has traditionally associated women with holding a 'natural' propensity for care work, which has led to disregarding the efforts and the emotional labour that care work involves (Hochschild, 2012).

Moreover, empirical research has stressed that recruiters may select migrant candidates depending on the stereotypical views they have on national origins (MacKenzie, 2009; Findlay et al., 2013). According to this literature, citizenship or pretended country of origin are used as proxies to differentiate between migrant workers. To be considered "good workers" (MacKenzie, 2009), candidates need to fit employers' national and racialised stereotypes.

However, recent publications have emphasised that there is a need to study the impact of essentialism in the labour market from an intersectional perspective (Dyer et al., 2010; Alberti & Iannuzzi, 2020). Indeed, essentialism based on racialisation interacts with essentialism based on class and gender, which results in naturalising skills in specific bodies and limiting access to jobs. The few empirical studies that have analysed essentialism in the labour market from an intersectional perspective have focused on the domestic and care work sector (Scrinzi, 2013; Abrantes, 2014), nursing (Likupe, 2015), the hospitality and tourism industry (Dyer et al., 2010; Swan & Flowers, 2018; Alberti & Iannuzzi, 2020), and show business (Dean, 2008). Rather than concentrating on a specific sector, the book proposes to analyse the issue focusing on a specific profile of workers, namely that of migrant women with tertiary education. This approach permits us to tackle essentialism in areas of the labour market that have been understudied.

Agency and Coping Strategies Scholars have highlighted that research on essentialism has often approached oppressed groups as passive recipients of these harms (Rosenthal et al., 2020). Moreover, migrant women are often depicted in the literature as being vulnerable victims who lack agency (Parolari, 2019). To contrast this stereotyping representation, the book proposes to study how migrant women cope, resist and eventually challenge essentialism and labour market stratifications. Scholars have pointed out that the migration projects are multiple and differentiated, based on gender, age, country of origin, and networks, and also depend on the historical context (Tognetti Bordogna, 2012). In this regard, Raghuram (2008) has highlighted that women with tertiary education hold social and cultural capital that they often intend to value and enhance in the country of destination. Moreover, researchers have shown that the failure to find work in the field of education might lead to depression (Killian & Manohar, 2015) and women might identify their migration with a loss of socio-professional status (Riaño, 2012).

Researchers have identified different strategies implemented by migrant women with tertiary education to cope with downward mobility (Liversage, 2009; Vianello, 2014). The book proposes to complete these typologies by analysing how migrant women with tertiary education cope with, resist, and eventually challenge both essentialism and labour market stratifications.

* * *

Research Questions Overall, the chapter has introduced the theoretical lenses that are used to analyse the positioning and the challenges of migrant women with tertiary education. It has also critically defined the terms that are used in the literature, especially the concept of skilled migration. Moreover, it has reviewed the literature concerning migrant women with tertiary education and their access to employment, highlighting some of the gaps that need further research. It is based on these omissions that the research questions are constructed. More specifically, the book answers the following questions:

- How do migrant women with tertiary education, recruiters and social workers perceive employment stratifications and essentialism in the labour market? (Chap. 3)

- How does essentialism influence the assessment of skills? More specifically, how does essentialism interfere with the evaluation of diplomas, experience gained abroad, language, and soft skills? (Chap. 4)
- What strategies are implemented by migrant women with tertiary education to cope, resist and eventually challenge stratifications and essentialism? (Chap. 5)

References

Abrantes, M. (2014). 'I know it sounds nasty and stereotyped': Searching for the competent domestic worker. *Gender, Work and Organization, 21*(5), 427–442.

Alberti, G., & Iannuzzi, F. E. (2020). Embodied intersectionality and the intersectional management of hotel labour: The everyday experiences of social differentiation in customer-oriented work. *Gender, Work and Organization, 27*(6), 1165–1180.

Almeida, S., & Fernando, M. (2017). Making the cut: Occupation-specific factors influencing employers in their recruitment and selection of immigrant professionals in the information technology and accounting occupations in regional Australia. *The International Journal of Human Resource Management, 28*(6), 880–912.

Arulampalam, W., Booth, A. L., & Bryan, M. L. (2007). Is there a glass ceiling over Europe? Exploring the gender pay gap across the wage distribution. *ILR Review, 60*(2), 163–186.

Balbo, L. (1978). La doppia presenza. *Inc, 32*(8), 3–11.

Bolzani, D., Crivellaro, F., & Grimaldi, R. (2021). Highly skilled, yet invisible. The potential of migrant women with a STEMM background in Italy between intersectional barriers and resources. *Gender, Work and Organization, 28*(6), 2132–2157.

Bonilla Silva, E. (2014). *Racism without racists.* Rowman & Littlefield.

Boucher, A. K. (2020). How 'skill' definition affects the diversity of skilled immigration policies. *Journal of Ethnic and Migration Studies, 46*(12), 2533–2550.

Bourdieu, P. (1993). Esprits d'Etat. Genèse et structure du champ bureaucratique. *Actes de la recherche en sciences sociales, 96*(1), 49–62.

Brandi, M. C. (2010). Le migrazioni qualificate dall'Europa dell'Est verso l'Italia. *Studi Emigrazione, XLVII*, 179.

Browne, I., & Misra, J. (2003). The intersection of gender and race in the labor markets. *Annual Review of Sociology, 29*, 487–513.

Bussola, M., & Pelliccia, A. (2012). Le parole nel racconto dei migranti polacchi altamente qualificati. Territori Sociologici, 11.

Castles, S., & Miller, M. J. (2009). *The age of migration: International population movements in the modern world*. Palgrave Macmillan.

Chiswick, B. R., & Miller, P. W. (2009). The international transferability of immigrants' human capital. *Economics of Education Review, 28*(2), 162–169.

Coccia, B., & Pittau, F. (Eds.). (2016). *Le migrazione qualificate in Italia. Ricerche, statistiche, prospettive*. Centro Studi e Ricerche IDOS.

Cossée, C., Miranda, A., Ouali, N., & Séhili, D. (Eds.). (2012). *Le genre au cœur des migrations*. Petra.

Crenshaw, K. (1989). Demarginalizing the intersection of race and sex: A black feminist critique of antidiscrimination doctrine, feminist theory and antiracist politics. *University of Chicago Legal Forum, 140*, 139–167.

Cuban, S. (2013). *Deskilling migrant women in the global care industry*. Palgrave Macmillan.

Daadouch, C. (2007). Des discriminations plus légitimes que d'autres? Les emplois fermés aux étrangers. *Journal du droit des jeunes, 266*(6), 35–36.

Dean, D. (2008). No human resource is an island: Gendered, racialized access to work as a performer. *Gender, Work and Organization, 15*(2), 161–181.

Dumitru, S. (2019). Travailleuses domestiques et autres stéréotypes sur les femmes migrantes. *L'Economie politique, 4*, 59–71.

Dyer, S., McDowell, L., & Batnitzky, A. (2010). The impact of migration on the gendering of service work: The case of a West London hotel. *Gender, Work and Organization, 17*, 635–657.

European Council. (2009). EU Council Directive 2009/50/EC of 25 May 2009 on the conditions of entry and residence of third-country nationals for the purposes of highly qualified employment. Available at: https://eur-lex.europa.eu/legal-content/EN/TXT/?uri=celex%3A32009L0050

Fassin, D., & Fassin, E. (2006). *De la question sociale à la question raciale? Représenter la société française*. La Découverte.

Findlay, A., McCollum, D., Shubin, S., Apsite, E., & Krisjane, Z. (2013). The role of recruitment agencies in imagining and producing the 'good' migrant. *Social & Cultural Geography, 14*(2), 145-167.

Fresnoza-Flot, A., & Shinozaki, K. (2017). Transnational perspectives on intersecting experiences: Gender, social class and generation among southeast Asian migrants and their families. *Journal of Ethnic and Migration Studies, 43*(6), 867–884.

Goffman, E. (1990). *Stigma. Notes on the management of spoiled identity*. Penguin.
Grigoleit, G. (2010). Making a career? The integration of highly skilled female migrants into the German job market. *APPAM International Conference Migration,* Netherlands, February 18–20.
Grigoleit-Richter, G. (2017). Highly skilled and highly mobile? Examining gendered and ethnicised labour market conditions for migrant women in STEM-professions in Germany. *Journal of Ethnic and Migration Studies, 43*(16), 2738–2755.
Groot, W., & Maassen Van Den Brink, H. (2000). Overeducation in the labor market: A meta-analysis. *Economics of Education Review, 19*(2), 149–158.
Gropas, R., & Bartolini, L. (2016). Southern European highly skilled female migrants in male-dominated sectors in times of crisis: A look into the it and engineering sectors In *High-skill migration and recession* (pp. 160–192). Palgrave Macmillan.
Grosfoguel, R., Oso, L., & Christou, A. (2015). 'Racism', intersectionality and migration studies: Framing some theoretical reflections. *Identities, 22*(6), 635–652.
Grosz, E. (1990). A note on essentialism and difference. In S. Gunew (Ed.), *Feminist knowledge: Critique and construct* (pp. 332–344). Routledge.
Hochschild, A. R. (2012). *The managed heart: Commercialization of human feeling*. University of California Press.
Hondagneu-Sotelo, P. (Ed.). (2003). *Gender and U.S. immigration: Contemporary trends*. University of California Press.
Jentjens, S. (2021). Je ne parle pas français—So what? The impact of language on skilled German migrant women's employment in France. *International Journal of Cross Cultural Management, 21*(1), 71–93.
Killian, C., & Manohar, N. N. (2015). Highly skilled immigrant Women's labor market access. *Social Currents, 3*(2), 138–159.
Kofman, E. (2012). Gender and skilled migration in Europe. *Cuadernos de Relaciones Laborales, 30*(1), 63–89.
Kofman, E., & Raghuram, P. (2015). *Gendered migrations and global social reproduction*. Palgrave Macmillan UK.
Likupe, G. (2015). Experiences of African nurses and the perception of their managers in the NHS. *Journal of Nursing Management, 23*(2), 231–241.
Liversage, A. (2009). Vital conjunctures, shifting horizons: High-skilled female immigrants looking for work. *Work, Employment & Society, 23*(1), 120–141.
MacKenzie, F. (2009). The rhetoric of the "good worker" versus the realities of employer's use and the experiences of migrant workers. *Work, Employment & Society, 23*(1), 142–159.

Mezzadra, S., & Neilson, B. (2013). *Border as method, or, the multiplication of labor*. Duke University Press.

Morris, L. (2001). The ambiguous terrain of rights: Civic stratification in Italy's emergent immigration regime. *International Journal of Urban and Regional Research, 25*(3), 497–516.

Moscovici, S. (2015). *La psychanalyse, son image et son public*. Presses universitaires de France.

Ndiaye, P. (2008). *La condition noire. Essai sur une minorité française*. Calmann-Lévy.

Parolari, P. (2019). Stereotipi di genere, discriminazioni contro le donne e vulnerabilità come disempowerment. Riflessioni sul ruolo del diritto. *About Gender, 8*(15), 90–117.

Parreñas, R. (2020). *Servants of globalization: Migration and domestic work*. Stanford University Press.

Petrovich Njegosh, T., & Scacchi, A. (2012). *Parlare di razza. La lingua del colore tra Italia e Stati Uniti*. Ombre corte.

Portes, A., & Bach, R. L. (1985). *Latin journey: Cuban and Mexican immigrants in the United States*. University of California Press.

Purkayastha, D., & Bircan, T. (2021). Present but not counted: Highly skilled migrant women in Belgium. *Journal of Ethnic and Migration Studies*, 1–19.

Quraishi, M., & Philburn, R. (2015). *Researching racism*. Sage.

Raghuram, P. (2008). Migrant women in male-dominated sectors of the labour market: A research agenda. *Population, Space and Place, 14*, 43–57.

Riaño, Y. (2012). The invisibility of family in studies of skilled migration and brain drain. *Diversities, 14*(1), 25–44.

Ricci, A., Crivellaro, F., & Bolzani, D. (2021). Perceived employability of highly skilled migrant women in STEM: Insights from labor market intermediaries' professionals. *Administrative Sciences, 11*(1), 7.

Rodriguez, J. K., & Scurry, T. (2019). Female and foreign: An intersectional exploration of the experiences of skilled migrant women in Qatar. *Gender, Work and Organization, 26*(4), 480–500.

Romens, A.-I. (2021). Disentangling interlocking regimes in the biographies of migrant mothers with tertiary education. *European Journal of Cultural and Political Sociology, 8*(4), 402–426.

Rosenthal, L., Overstreet, N. M., Khukhlovich, A., Brown, B. E., Godfrey, C.-J., & Albritton, T. (2020). Content of, sources of, and responses to sexual stereotypes of black and Latinx women and men in the United States: A qualitative intersectional exploration. *Journal of Social Issues, 76*(4), 921–948.

Sayad, A. (2016). *La double absence. Des illusions de l'émigré aux souffrances de l'immigré*. Seuil.

Scrinzi, F. (2013). *Genre, migrations et emplois domestiques en France et en Italie. Construction de la non-qualification et de l'altérité ethnique*. Pétra.

Shinozaki, K. (2014). Career strategies and spatial mobility among skilled migrants in Germany: The role of gender in the work-family interaction. *Tijdschrift voor Economische en Sociale Geografie, 105*(5), 526–541.

Shinozaki, K. (2017). Gender and citizenship in academic career progression: An intersectional, meso-scale analysis in German higher education institutions. *Journal of Ethnic and Migration Studies, 43*(8), 1325–1346.

Sirna, F. (2020). Femmes migrantes dans le secteur hospitalier en région Sud pendant la pandémie de la Covid-19. *Hommes & migrations, 1331*, 38–47.

Swan, E., & Flowers, R. (2018). Lasting impressions: Ethnic food tour guides and body work in southwestern Sydney. *Gender, Work and Organization, 25*(1), 24–41.

Tajfel, H., & Turner, J. C. (1986). The social identity theory of inter-group behavior. In S. Worchel & W. Austin (Eds.), *Psychology of intergroup relations* (pp. 7–24). Nelson-Hall.

Terray, E. (2008). Pourquoi partent-ils? In C. Rodier & E. Terray (Eds.), *Immigration: fantasmes et réalités. Pour une alternative à la fermeture des frontières*. La Découverte.

Toffanin, A. M. (2015). *Controcanto. Donne latinoamericane tra violenza e riconoscimento*. Guerini Scientifica.

Tognetti Bordogna, M. (2012). *Donne e percorsi migratori. Per una sociologia delle migrazioni*. Franco Angeli.

Triandafyllidou, A., & Isaakyan, I. (Eds.). (2016). *High skill migration and recession: Gendered perspectives*. Springer.

Tsing, A. (2009). Supply chains and the human condition. *Rethinking Marxism, 21*(2), 148–176.

Unesco. (2012). *International standard classification of education, ISCED 2011*. UNESCO Institute for Statistics.

Vasey, H. (2021). Deconstructing skills in the stratification of migration governance. In H. Carmel, K. Lenner, & R. Paul (Eds.), *Handbook on the governance and the politics of migration* (pp. 173–184). Edward Elgar.

Vianello, F. A. (2009). *Migrando sole*. Legami transnazionali tra Ucraina e Italia, Franco Angeli.

Vianello, F. A. (2014). Ukrainian migrant workers in Italy: Coping with and reacting to downward mobility. *Central and Eastern European Migration Review, 3*(1), 85–98.

Williams, F. (2010). Migration and care: Themes, concepts and challenges. *Social Policy and Society, 9*(3), 385–396.

Wojczewski, S., Pentz, S., Blacklock, C., Hoffmann, K., Peersman, W., Nkomazana, O., & Kutalek, R. (2015). African female physicians and nurses in the global care chain: Qualitative explorations from five destination countries. *PLoS One, 10*(6), e0129464. https://doi.org/10.1371/journal.pone.0129464

Wolkowitz, C. (2006). *Bodies at work*. Sage.

Wong, M. (2014). Geographies and strategies of caregiving among skilled Ghanaian migrant women. *Women's Studies International Forum, 42*, 28.

Yeates, N. (2009). *Globalizing care economies and migrant workers: Explorations in global care chains*. Palgrave Macmillan.

Zhou, M., & Logan, J. R. (1998). Returns on human Capital in Ethnic Enclaves: New York City's Chinatown. *American Sociological Review, 54*(5), 809–833.

3

"First the Europeans, Then Maybe the Filipinas, Then you". Perceiving Stratifications and Essentialism

Rosella was studying medicine in the Democratic Republic of Congo when she left because students were being targeted by the military regime. It was becoming impossible for her to finish her academic years as her university was frequently forced to shut down. Rosella arrived in Veneto at the beginning of the 1980s, through a Catholic Church channel, to continue her studies. Despite her motivation, it took her several years to obtain her final degree, as she had to combine her studies with work and care for her newly born son. Before starting to work in her field of studies, she had several jobs in the cleaning and care industries. Rosella, who has lived in the region for almost forty years, believed that there was a turning point in migrants' access to employment in the 1990s. From that period, she felt that Africans started feeling "skin diversity". Rosella described the progressive stratification of the labour market, indicating that workers, and especially migrant women, had priority in hiring depending on their nationality.

> *When I arrived [in Italy] in 1982, we were very few [migrant women]. We could find work as domestic workers[...]. But when there was the boom of immigration, around the 1990s, there then, especially we Africans, we started*

A.-I. Romens, *Deconstructing Essentialism*,
https://doi.org/10.1007/978-3-031-14399-1_3

to feel the diversity of the skin. So, if someone shows up, when the Eastern [European] women arrived, when the Filipinas arrived: 'No, first them, first the Europeans, then maybe the Filipinas, then you [the African women]'. So, [that is when] started precisely this mistrust towards Africa, towards Africans. (Rosella, born in the Democratic Republic of Congo, physician, Italy).

In her account, Rosella made explicit reference to the gendered and racialised stratifications of the labour market, highlighting that essentialist processes were targeting African migrant women and limiting their access to jobs. Following her observations, we can wonder how local labour markets are stratified and how essentialism based on racialisation, gender, and class influences the recruiters' decision-making, limiting the access that migrant women have to employment. This chapter aims at exploring the issue by cross-referencing the perspectives among the stakeholders involved in the process of accessing employment, namely migrant women with tertiary education, recruiters, and social workers.

3.1 Feeling Essentialised: Migrant Women's Perspectives

To begin with, I explore how migrant women perceive labour market stratifications and how they feel that essentialism influences their access to jobs. The first part focuses on the perspectives of women born in countries of Sub-Saharan Africa; the second analyses the views of women born in European non-EU countries.

Black Migrant Women and White Walls

Both in my French and Italian fieldworks, interviewees born in Sub-Saharan Africa stressed that the fact of being Black was anything but an advantage to find employment commensurate with their graduate degree status. "There are so many prejudices" explained Rosamel, who was born in Cameroon and was working as a physiotherapist in Veneto at the time of the interview. In Alsace, Callaia, who worked as a nurse, mentioned the specific stereotypes with which she felt Africans were associated. "They believe we are lazy", she said. As a result, Callaia felt she needed to work twice as much as others would.

In both regions, interviewees indicated that they felt there was an invisible wall that prevented Black migrant women from accessing graduate employment. This impression was based on their job-hunting experience as well as on that of their family members, friends and acquaintances. Both in Alsace and Veneto, it happened that migrant women were told by recruiters that they would not get the job because they were Black. In Italy, this is what happened to Raisa, who was born in Cameroon and held an Italian master's degree in communication sciences and marketing. Since Raisa graduated, she had struggled to find employment in her field. When I met her, she was occasionally working as a cultural mediator. Raisa stressed that she has had several job interviews. In one of them, she was told that the employer "did not want to *colour*" the company.

> *I did a lot of interviews after graduation. In some cases, they tell you: "You know the world, for example of the [name of the company], we don't want to colour the environment. We need a little... It's a bit stiff. I tell you clearly because it is useless to tell you that as soon as we need someone, we call you". That's the truth. And unfortunately, you turn and go out with such despair.* (Raisa, born in Cameroon, cultural mediator, Italy).

Cassia had a similar experience in Alsace. She was born in Senegal, where she obtained a bachelor's in management and ICT and worked for over six years as an administrative assistant. She moved to France to join her partner, expecting to continue her professional career. When I met her, she had been in Alsace for two years but was still struggling to find employment in line with her studies. Cassia indicated that she was once called for an interview as a management assistant. During the meeting, the recruiter told her that the fact of being Black, coupled with that of not having a French degree, would make it difficult to find a job in her field.

In both regions, Black migrant women with tertiary education also reported that they felt they tended to be confined in "subaltern" positions, especially in feminised jobs at the bottom of the employment structure. While they were regularly being rejected for positions requiring graduate degrees, these women felt that when applying for jobs with low social recognition, they had more chances to be accepted. Rosanna, who was born in Cameroon and studied economics in Italy, stressed that she applied several times for positions in line with her studies but never got a reply. Conversely, she had managed to find employment as a cleaner, and more recently as a care assistant.

> *As a graduate, they will never hire me […]. Instead as a care assistant, as a cleaner yes, you see. And we [African migrants] say to ourselves: "yes, this is what they believe we can do".* (Rosanna, born in Cameroon, care assistant, Italy).

Cassia, who graduated in management and IT in Senegal and lived in Alsace, had similar feelings. The woman was especially critical of the person that was following her case at Pôle Emploi, the French agency in charge of providing support to unemployed workers. As a registered unemployed, Cassia should have been able to follow training supported by the institution. She wanted to pursue a course connected to banking, but her adviser at Pôle Emploi never answered. Conversely, when she asked to pursue a training programme for being a childcare assistant, he processed her request in a couple of weeks. Out of this experience, Cassia concluded that women like her were perceived to be "only good" for "subaltern jobs".

> *I didn't think it was going to be as hard as it is, that it was going to be… as discriminating as it is. That's it. But, they make you know it outright… Yeah, they tell you "I'll call you back", and then there's no feedback. But on the other hand, when I wanted to do the childcare thing, then it did not hang there. You come, they take you straightaway. At a push, we are only good for that, either to do… to sweep, to deal with… subaltern jobs, yeah.* (Cassia, born in Senegal, unemployed, France).

In both contexts, Black migrant women stressed that they felt they were perceived as low-skilled workers. As a result, they had the feeling that interlocutors, such as recruiters, but also patients or clients, were sceptical or surprised when they learned that they were graduates or that they were experienced professionals. For instance, Callaia who worked as a nurse in Alsace told me that, when she worked with a white colleague, it often happened that patients asked questions to the latter, ignoring Callaia, even though she had a higher professional position.

Similarly, in Veneto, Rosamel, who worked as a physiotherapist, mentioned the surprise she created with recruiters and secretaries, while she was looking for employment. By that time Rosamel already held an Italian university degree and had working experience in the region. When leaving her resume, she often heard that spokespersons were surprised and asked: "But are you a physiotherapist?", "How have you done it?".

The previous paragraphs have highlighted that both in Veneto and Alsace, migrant women who were perceived as Black, faced essentialism based on the intersection of racialisation and gender which confined them to jobs with low social recognition. However, it also happened that they accessed intermediary positions in specific sectors. For instance, Callaia was working as a nurse in Alsace and Rosamel as a physiotherapist in Veneto. As further detailed below, fieldwork highlighted that in both contexts, Black migrant women might access intermediate and graduate positions in specific sectors, such as those involving social reproduction (Kofman & Raghuram, 2015).

Another relevant observation that was mentioned by women from Sub-Saharan Africa, regarded the institutional challenges they faced when accessing employment. These obstacles concerned both the Italian and the French areas of fieldwork. For instance, in the Italian context, Rosella mentioned the institutional barriers that she had faced in her career. As mentioned, Rosella was born in the Democratic Republic of Congo and moved to Veneto by the beginning of the 1980s. Once she had finished her university career in Italy, she was successful in passing the State exam for physicians. Meanwhile, she explained that a new law was adopted that prevented non-EU citizens from registering with the Italian medical association. As a result, she was not authorised to work as a physician. "The discrimination that becomes law is ugly", said Rosella. Fortunately for Rosella, the norm was revoked a few years later. She could register with the medical association and started working as a physician.

> *If I meet a person in the street who tells me… he can tell me everything, I can bear racism… but the thing that hurts me the most is that one, you know, when the State legalised discrimination.* (Rosella, born in the Democratic Republic of Congo, physician, Italy).

When it comes to comparing both areas, it is interesting to note that interviewees in Italy tended to have an idealised image of France as being more open towards African migrants. Access to low and intermediary positions was mentioned as an example of the contrast between both countries. For instance, Rada, who was born in Cameroon and lived in Italy, indicated that she had been in France for holidays, and noticed that there were Black taxi drivers, cashiers, and public officials. "Here, in Italy", she said, "you can [go] to a thousand of supermarkets, you will never see a Black cashier". When I told Callaia, who worked as a nurse in Alsace, that some interviewees in Veneto perceived France as providing more opportunities for Black women, she said that "it's not true". Callaia found that "it [was] only more insidious" and gave further examples of how she was continuously being treated as "other" at work.

Another relevant difference in the accounts of the interviewees according to the research context regarded their relative employment positions compared to other migrant groups. In Veneto, interviewees explicitly referred to stratifications according to country of birth and skin colour. As mentioned in the opening of the chapter, Rosella raised the issue by observing how stratifications have changed over time. Conversely, in Alsace, participants born in Sub-Saharan Africa compared their access to the labour market to that of white locals and children of migration. They did not refer to the positioning of other migrant women nor stratifications based on migrants' country of birth. The views of migrant women with tertiary education that were born in countries of Sub-Saharan Africa are summarised in Table 3.1.

Table 3.1 Views of women born in Sub-Saharan African countries on the impact of essentialism in accessing employment, according to the research context

Similarities between the Italian and French local labour markets	Differences between the Italian and French local labour markets
• Skin colour matters when accessing employment • stereotypes about African candidates prevent them from accessing jobs • Women born in sub Saharan African countries are perceived as being "only good" for "subaltern jobs", regardless of their educational background • Institutional obstacles prevent migrant women from accessing the job they want	Italian local labour market (Veneto): • Stratifications based on the nationality of migrants and racialisation are visible • Interviewees in Italy perceived that intermediary jobs were more accessible in France French local labour market (Alsace): • Racialisation of black migrant women is more 'insidious' (compared to Italy) • Interviewees emphasised differences in accessing jobs between migrants and locals (and did not refer to a hierarchy between migrants according to their nationality)

The Otherness of Women from European Non-EU Countries

The interaction with women from European non-EU countries stressed that, although they tended not to feel explicitly racialised as non-white in local labour markets, they were also subject to forms of essentialism. In Italy, migrant women with tertiary education born in European non-EU countries referred to the way they felt they were being perceived. For instance, Viola, who was born in Russia where she used to work as a professor and financial director, contrasted the respected position she had in Russia with the denigration she was facing in Veneto. She felt *otherised* and suffered from being devalued.

> *So, now, everything is different. I became a migrant from Eastern Europe, let's say, little, little respected, little... let's say that people sometimes talk to me like... like an idiot absolutely. The last thing, the general practitioner was*

talking to me, as if… as if I were an idiot. This is difficult. (Viola, born in Russia, unemployed, Italy).

Like women from Sub-Saharan Africa, women from European non-EU countries who lived in Italy also referred to implicit hierarchies based on the country of birth. For instance, Veronica, who was born in Ukraine, distinguished the way migrants were perceived depending on whether they came from a powerful country in the international arena.

I realised, however, that [in Veneto] I am an extracomunitaria.[1] *But I am not a non-EU citizen from the United States who maybe has a certain [position]. But I am a non-EU citizen from Ukraine, that here are [perceived as] carers, who take care of the old women, or the young girls who are prostitutes.* (Veronica, born in Ukraine, administrative assistant, Italy).

Veronica provided a contrasting picture of the way she felt Ukrainian women were being perceived in Veneto. On the one hand, she felt that Ukrainian women were in a disadvantaged position as they tended to be associated with stigmatised jobs with low social recognition, such as those of in-home carers and sex workers. Her perception illustrates how essentialism intersects gender and racialisation with class, signified by specific jobs. On the other hand, Veronica also found that Ukrainians and more generally women from Eastern European countries were perceived as holding a high work ethic. Although Veronica estimated that the stereotyping contributed to her being retained for a position as a business manager, she still had to face the violence of being inserted into a racialised and gendered labour market, in which essentialism is made explicit.

[The manager] said: "I appreciate the girls from the East because I feel they have a great sense of responsibility, of working". He often sees Italians talking, drinking coffee, talking, drinking coffee, and going out of the workplace (Veronica, born in Ukraine, administrative assistant, Italy).

[1] Ambrosini (2009) stresses that the expression *extracomunitari* (non EU citizen) is mainly used in the Italian debate to refer to foreigners from countries which are perceived as being poor.

Similarly, Winika, who was also born in Ukraine and worked as a pizza maker in Italy, also mentioned explicit hierarchies based on nationality. She referred to a specific job interview, during which the recruiter, who would, later on, hire her, indicated he preferred *Slavs* over candidates "from Africa" or Muslims. Like Veronica, although Winika was hired, she also had to face the violence of being inserted into a stratified labour market.

> *I have heard more than once, when they say "We prefer you, the Slavs, than those from Africa, or Muslims and so on". But this [racism], let's say, this is not part of my personal experience. [...] [Incidents] have happened to me, but that does not depend on the company or the manager, or on the people who hire me. It is these everyday people that you meet, and who talk to you. That work hasn't been hard, but it's hard to bear the people next to you. There is racism.* (Winika, born in Ukraine, pizzaiola, Italy).

In Alsace, fieldwork also gave a contrasting picture of the essentialist processes that targeted European women from non-EU countries. There was a gap between those who felt concerned with positive stereotypes, and those who felt stigmatised for being foreigners. Whether positive or negative, these stereotypes always involved forms of essentialism. Like Veronica in Veneto, Abelia, who was born in Russia and worked as a librarian in Alsace, had the impression that Eastern Europeans had the reputation of being "good workers", which facilitated her access to a position as a sales assistant. Conversely, Azalea, who was also born in Russia, found that her co-nationals were not that privileged in the local labour market. Based on her own experience and that of friends, she believed that French private companies were quite reluctant to hire foreigners, including Eastern Europeans.

Azalea found that another obstacle concerned the French regulations. She explained that employers who wanted to hire a non-EU citizen were expected to prove they had not found a French or an EU candidate for the position. The practice that Azalea mentioned was introduced in 2011 through the so-called *Guéant circular*. Although the text was revoked, norms continued to discourage the recruitment and selection of non-EU citizens, as employers needed to pay a specific tax and had additional paperwork to fill in. In practice, the French norms continued to discriminate against non-EU candidates when accessing the labour market.

> *I was a little bit naïve [when moving to France], in that sense because I thought I would find a company, a French company, which could hire me, but then I realised it's not possible at all, as French companies have very strict requirements concerning foreigners. To hire a foreigner, not from the EU, they have to really prove my added value, they have to organise interviews with French people. And only if French [candidates] are not suitable for the job, they can hire me, make all of these requests for my visa.* (Azalea, born in Russia, administrative assistant, France).

Like Azalea, Amapola, who was born in Albania and worked as an administrative assistant in Alsace, also emphasised the role of migration policies in preventing migrant women from accessing employment. Amapola used to have one-year permits for family reasons and felt that employers did not want to hire her because they were sceptical regarding whether she would obtain a new residence permit.

> *I was going twice a week [to the job agencies]: "Hello, do you have something for me?" (laugh). I would say to myself, I have nothing to lose. And sometimes, they would tell me "oh yes can I…", each time there was a new person, "can I have your residence permit?". They would see it, but sometimes it was halfway, so I only had six months left. "Yes, but you have a six-month residence permit, it is difficult to…". And I would say, "Yeah, but I don't intend to separate or divorce, that's how they are delivered. That doesn't mean that… I would have it automatically. Normally I have it. There are no worries". I don't know if that was what… restrained [them], but it became at a certain point… I remember, I was living it very badly. I was desperate, really.* (Amapola, born in Albania, administrative assistant, France).

The accounts of Azalea and Amapola stressed that migratory policies and norms on hiring limit the access that graduate migrant women have to the labour market. Moreover, as these policies specially target citizens from non-EU countries, they strengthen the reluctance that recruiters might have towards candidates from this area. In the end, these policies contribute to the stratification of the local labour market, based on racialisation and gender, and reinforce the internal boundaries between migrants and non-migrants (Amelina & Horvath, 2020). Faced with a local labour market that appeared to be closed to foreigners, both Amapola and Azalea decided to look for opportunities within the international organisations that are present in Alsace. Access to these institutions will be further explored in Sect. 3.3. of this chapter.

When it comes to contrasting the outcomes in both regions, it is worth noting that in Veneto interviewees were more eloquent about the essentialist processes that targeted them, highlighting that stratifications according to nationality, were made explicit by recruiters. Like the women from Sub-Saharan Africa in Italy, those from European non-EU countries also compared their position with that of women from other areas. Conversely in Alsace, women from European non-EU countries did not describe explicit stratifications based on nationality. Nonetheless, they also indicated that they were concerned with forms of essentialism. Compared to Veneto, interviewees in Alsace seemed more concerned about the legal and administrative constraints that were preventing them from having full access to graduate positions. Overall, it was the practices of private actors that were at the core of the concerns in Veneto, while in France women from European non-EU countries were more worried about how segregation was institutionalised. Table 3.2 summarises their perspectives.

Table 3.2 Views of women born in European non-EU countries on the impact of essentialism in accessing employment, according to the research context

Italian local labour market (Veneto)	• Women born in European (non-Eu) countries feel they are being otherised • Women born in European (non-Eu) countries are target of different forms of stereotyping regarding their ability to work and the sectors in which they could work • These women feel there are specific labour stratifications based on nationality and that employers appreciate or disregard workers capacities depending on their country of birth
French local labour market (Alsace)	• Women born in European (non-Eu) countries are target of different forms of stereotyping regarding their ability to work • Recruiters have prejudices regarding foreigners in general (including European non EU candidates) • Restrictive norms on hirings (i.e. Priority to EU candidates) and migratory policies (i.e. Short-term family permits) have a negative impact on these women's access to jobs • Positions within international organisations are perceived as being more accessible

3.2 Recruiters' and Social Workers' Perspectives

After analysing the perspective of migrant women, the following section studies how labour market gatekeepers perceive essentialism and stratifications. In this regard, I expected that recruiters would have a high level of reserve regarding essentialism in the labour market, as they were probably aware of the social and legal condemnation of racism and other forms of discrimination (Fassin, 2006: 143). Although comments by human resources managers and social workers varied, fieldwork partially confirmed the preview's hypothesis. Nevertheless, the research method, namely that of conducting narrative interviews, permitted me to put participants at ease so as to describe specific recruitment processes referring to essentialism and labour market stratifications. The first paragraphs analyse the perspective of labour market gatekeepers in Alsace, while the second focuses on Veneto.

Migrant Women's Otherness in the French Context

In Alsace, positions of recruiters and social workers on the impact of essentialism in accessing jobs can be arrayed along a continuum that goes from *denegating* (Fassin, 2006) the impact of essentialism in recruitment and selection, at one extreme of the continuum, to acknowledging that essentialism has an impact on access to jobs, at the other extreme. The main positions of labour market gatekeepers in the French local labour market are synthesised in Scheme 3.1.

At one extreme of the continuum was Drake who worked for an intermediary agency recruiting graduate professionals for top positions. He asked me not to record the interview and was concerned about the outcome of my research. Although Drake acknowledged that "some" recruiters had prejudices and "some" companies in Alsace were "racist", he saw these practices as being isolated. Drake also mentioned the practice of using *BBR, Bleu-Blanc-Rouge,* as an eligibility criterion but argued that it was no longer in practice. The term refers to the French flag and indicates that selected candidates need to be not only French but more specifically that they have to look "white" (Fassin, 2006: 142).

Scheme 3.1 Views of labour market gatekeepers on the impact of essentialism in accessing employment in Alsace (France)

• Denegating essentialism (victims tend to exaggerate), although using "culture" as an eligibility criteria	• Candidates are perceived differently according to nationality • Perception changes over time	• Essentialism based on the intersection of gender, country of birth and racialisation matters in the selection and recruitment process • Migrant women associated with conservative models of femininity have easier access to feminised jobs

Despite indicating that essentialist criteria did not count in the selection process, Drake referred to "culture" as an eligibility criterion. For instance, he mentioned specific attitudes that were more or less compatible with "company cultures", stressing that he would not hire an "outgoing" person in an "introverted" business context. Meanwhile, he also referred to the "African culture" indicating that Africans were more "outgoing" and focused on collectivity. Therefore, we can wonder to what extent his perception of "African culture" interfered in the selection process.

Moreover, Drake also blamed victims of discrimination, indicating that he found they tended to exaggerate. More specifically, Drake used the noun "victimisation" to refer to the fact that, from his perspective, some candidates confined themselves to the role of "victims" and wrongly believed they were not being recruited because they were being discriminated against. From his perspective, the victims of discrimination who succeeded in finding jobs were those who accepted that some companies had prejudices and looked for open-minded employers.

The comments of Drake echo Didier Fassin (2006)'s analysis of the French Republican model and the trend since the 2000s to *denegate* discriminations. According to the researcher, prejudices are too present to be denied entirely but too unethical to be named. As a result, discriminations tend to be diminished, and victims are delegitimised, insofar as it is believed that they exaggerate the impact of prejudices. Drake's example goes beyond that as victims are also those who are expected to act to overcome discriminations. Indeed, they are the ones who have to look for companies that are "open" and willing to hire them, while accepting that others might discriminate against them.

Dianella also worked as a recruiter in Alsace but adopted a different position. During the interview, she was more willing to speak about stratifications based on nationality and gender. For instance, she found that the country of birth matters but that the perception of third countries had evolved over time. "Italy does not frighten anymore", she observed, "I do not remember when Italians came to France and scared everyone because they were taking jobs, 70 or 50 years ago". At the time of the interview, Dianella found that women candidates continued to be seen differently according to nationality. She referred to a Colombian candidate that was recently hired for a graduate position in her company. Dianella found that it was easier for Colombian female candidates to be recruited as they were perceived as being *exotic.*[2] Conversely, she found it more challenging to get accepted for women from Northern Africa or the Middle East.

> *And for specific origins, well, I think managers can invent pretexts and they might not always be open-minded. [...]. Colombia, it went well, because Colombia, it's a little exotic. If the girl [candidate] had come from, well, Algeria, the Maghreb, a Maghreb country, or the Middle East, something like that, would it have been perceived - a Turkish - would it have been perceived in the same way? I don't know.* (Dianella, recruiter, France).

Social workers in Alsace were more eager than recruiters to speak about the challenges that migrant women faced when accessing the labour market, stressing that these women tended to be confined to positions at the bottom of the employment structure, regardless of their education level. For instance, Daphne, a social worker in Alsace, highlighted that positions in the hospitality, cleaning and eventually cooking sectors were among the jobs that migrant women tended to access, including those holding tertiary education. Daphne estimated that essentialist views that intersected pretended culture of origins with conservative models of femininity resulted in different access to employment. For example, the social worker found that Chechen women, in particular, were perceived as

[2] The perception of migrant women as being 'exotic' also involves essentialism as it will be stressed in the following chapter.

being "elegant", "coquette" and "submissive", while women from Sub-Saharan Africa tended to be seen as having a "strong personality". Consequently, Daphne found that essentialised perceptions of Chechen women that associated them with conservative models of femininity facilitated their access to feminised jobs such as cooks, dressmakers, or salespersons, while essentialist perceptions of Sub-Saharan African women would prevent them from accessing jobs in these sectors.

Moreover, and as far as graduates were concerned, Daphne felt that stigmatisation had a role to play in preventing migrants from accessing manager positions. Starting from her own experience as a child of Moroccan migrants, she found that she had faced obstacles in her career because of being "tanned" (*basané*). In Daphne's view, Eastern European women had an advantage because "physically", they corresponded to the "French standards". Through these examples, Daphne made explicit reference to the essentialist, racialising and gendered mechanisms that shaped the Alsatian local labour market.

> *I grew up in France; I did all my studies in France and even myself, I have faced challenges. Because we are tanned, more tanned than the Chechen woman. So, for us, it is already visible in our faces that we are not typical Europeans. The advantage that those of Eastern Europe have is that their profile well... physically, they already correspond to the French standards. They are blond, they might be avowed Muslims, or of a different culture, but physically they already answer the call. So it goes. And then, Sub-Saharan Africa, women are also famous for having strong character. So, at the manager level, we can say that it is harder because we will imagine that they will fit less easily into a mould.* (Daphne, social worker, France)

Explicit Preferences in the Italian Context

Recruiters and social workers in the Italian local labour market also made divergent comments on the issue, but none of them adopted Drake's position nor *denegated* discriminations. Their observations spread along a continuum from simple denial to the recognition of complex stratifications according to gender and nationality. The main positions of the labour market gatekeepers in the Italian local labour market are synthesised in Scheme 3.2.

Scheme 3.2 Views of labour market gatekeepers on the impact of essentialism in accessing employment in Veneto (Italy)

• No "preclusion", although using "culture" as an eligibility criteria	• Essentialism based on the intersection of gender, country of birth, racialisation and class matters in the selection and recruitment process • Essentialist criteria are made explicit by employers and recruiters

The comments of Shamrock, who worked for the HR department of a private company based in Veneto, can be placed in the first extreme of the continuum. From his perspective, there were "no preclusions" that would prevent foreign graduate women from accessing employment. Despite his denial, Shamrock also referred to "culture" as an eligibility criterion. Like Drake in Alsace, he indicated that foreign candidates "c[a]me from a different culture", and as such, he could not be sure that they would "share the company's values". In this case, also, we can wonder to what extent his perception of migrants' otherness interfered in the recruitment and selection process.

> *In our company, we already have, in the Italian factory, several foreign workers. Let's say that out of 170, a good 10%, yeah, is a foreigner. So we also have… in relevant positions such as the industrialisation manager, for example, is French… [we have] no preclusions. It is clear that in terms of communication and cultural impact it is never easy to find synergy, starting from the selection as well as from the perspective of sharing the values of the company, no, because coming from different cultures, there is not always… the same way of seeing things. So no kind of preclusions, this needs to be clear.* (Shamrock, recruiter, Italy).

Recruiters working for intermediary agencies in Veneto were more willing to speak about labour market stratifications. In this regard, De Rudder and Vourc'h (2006: 180) have pointed out that employment intermediaries occupy a privileged position from which they can observe discriminations in the labour market. Moreover, before conducting fieldwork, it was hypothesised that these actors would be keener to speak about discriminatory practices, as they could put the blame on their clients and present themselves as being external to such dynamics. The hypothesis was not confirmed in Alsace, where Drake preferred to diminish the importance of stratifications. However, the assumption worked out in Veneto, where intermediary recruiters described different forms of stratification. The contrast between intermediary recruiters in Alsace and Veneto could also be connected to the differences identified by Scrinzi (2013: 169), who estimates that recruitment, selection, training, and managing practices in France censure otherness, while in Italy, they tend to enlarge and stigmatise differences.

An example was provided by Sirelli, who had worked in an intermediary agency, where she mainly recruited and selected candidates for intermediary positions or jobs with low social recognition. She stressed that it came out that migrant female candidates were frequently graduates, including when applying for these types of jobs. Departing from her experience, Sirelli described the stratifications of the local labour market, giving the example of the hospitality industry. More specifically, the recruiter explained that depending on the position that opened, some nationalities were excluded while others were prioritised. For each specific job "there is a trend", she said, "to maintain the same nationalities".

From Sirelli's perspective, several reasons contributed to this strict stratification of the labour market, including essentialism which connected specific nationalities, countries of birth and racialised groups to characteristics that were appreciated or discredited by employers. Interestingly, the essentialist representations she mentioned were based on the intersection of racialisation and gender. For instance, Sirelli gave the example of Filipino men who were perceived as being "docile" and "kind", while Ukrainian women were seen as being "authoritative, strong, almost grouchy". Depending on the stereotype, candidates did or did not access the position.

Maybe there are also stereotypes, in the sense that a particular type of nationality. Maybe a certain kind of... how do you say, nationality is considered to have, I don't know, people with a more dominant personality, and others more submissive. The classic example is that of the Filipino who is described as docile and kind, and so on. If you think about it, for example, at the opposite extreme, the Ukrainian woman is generally seen as a woman that is… authoritative, strong, almost grouchy. No… yeah, in the collective imagination, in the labour imagination, that is, according to the context, there are, in short, there are stereotypes. (Sirelli, recruiter, Italy).

Sirelli also indicated that essentialist criteria could be explicitly mentioned by clients, who gave specific instructions on the nationalities they wanted or did not want to hire. When nationality exclusion was not explicitly stated, Sirelli explained that colleagues who knew the client indicated which nationalities had to be prioritised.

The colleagues let you know, the ones that have been working for a long time with clients, and the customers themselves tell you that. They tell you: 'I don't want [them], I don't want Moroccans'; there are those who don't want people of colour, in general, yeah, there are those who do not want women from the East, and so on. Of course, we know that all these things cannot be published. But then it is a job that gets done, precisely, in the process of skimming the curriculum. In short, one learns to do it, because you are told to do it, that's really something… often explicit, very explicit. (Sirelli, recruiter, Italy).

Similarly, Senecio, who had experience in headhunting, and as an intermediary recruiter for retirement homes, also indicated that there were "beliefs" concerning the "culture" of specific candidates that influenced recruitment and selection. Senecio referred to specific recruitment processes for nurses and care assistants, in which his supervisors explicitly asked him not to select African candidates, as they were perceived as being too abrupt. At the same time, he indicated that women from Eastern Europe tended to be excluded because they were seen as being too compliant and distant. He added that they were also negatively judged because they had an "in-home caregivers' attitude" (*badanti*).

The ladies from Eastern Europe who came to do the… interview for care assistants. Well… often they were disregarded, not only because of my opinion but also because of the opinion of other [members of the recruitment] commission. They were excluded [from the selection process] because they had this in-home caregivers' way of doing things. Some recruiters find that [this attitude] is 'inherent' in the culture of these… in the nationality of these people.

Well, and so yes, nationality sometimes influences [the selection process]. (Senecio, recruiter, Italy).

It is worth noting that the comment of Senecio crossed essentialism based on country of birth, gender and class. The "attitude" that was described corresponded to the *habitus* (Bourdieu, 1986) or embodied cultural capital, which strictly connects to social class. Habitus presupposes a process of incorporation that starts from early domestic education. It is converted into an integral part of the person. Its acquisition is disguised and functions as symbolic capital, meaning that it tends to be unrecognised as a form of capital and it is seen as a legitimate competence. As a result, the fact that recruiters disregarded in-home caregivers' attitudes gives the idea that they were negatively assessing what they associated with working-class habitus. As a result, it seemed that preferred candidates would be those who embodied middle-class habitus. This trend is further explored in Chap. 4.

The experience of social workers in Veneto echoed that of intermediary recruiters. They also highlighted that migrant women tend to be confined to positions at the bottom of the employment structure, regardless of their education level. When looking for internships or positions for the migrants they were following in the context of their job, social workers had to negotiate with employers who had specific requests in terms of gender, nationality, country of birth and racialisation. In this regard, Selena, a social worker in Veneto, had noticed that for each type of work, there was a selected nationality. "For instance", she said, "to work as a cleaning lady they ask us to find women from Sri Lanka, for in-home caregivers, they ask for Moldavians and Romanians". From Selena's perspective, Nigerians were those who faced more obstacles to accessing employment.

We have many women job seekers from Nigeria and for them nothing. It's very difficult for them to find work, even when they were doing very well in their country of birth. Because we have many service users from Lagos, who tell me 'in Lagos I was a teacher'. I understand, but here it is difficult to find even work as a cleaner. [...] So we have worked to organise training courses on cleaning, because there is this nationality preference, according to the job, even for the most unpretentious ones. (Selena, social worker, Italy).

Salma, who worked for a cooperative that offers support to migrants, made similar comments. Salma indicated that it was more difficult to access positions as in-house caregivers for women from Sub-Saharan Africa compared to women from other areas.

* * *

Overall, the accounts mentioned above highlighted that both in Alsace and Veneto essentialism based on gender and racialisation influences the appraisal of candidates. Compared to Veneto, in Alsace labour market gatekeepers tended to be less explicit on how the recruitment is influenced by essentialism. The differences between Alsace and Veneto in acknowledging or denying the essentialist processes at stake can be connected to the different models of addressing migrants' otherness. In France, the Republican model and recruiters' awareness of the legal and moral implications of using discriminatory criteria pushes them to diminish or silence their impact, which leads to what Fassin (2006: 147) identifies as '*denegation*': prejudices are too present to be denied entirely but too unethical to be named. Consequently, discrimination tends to be diminished, and victims are delegitimised, insofar as it is believed that they exaggerate the impact of prejudices. Conversely in Italy, our fieldwork highlights that the legal and social pressure to silence discrimination in accessing jobs is narrow, which leads to using these criteria more explicitly all along the recruitment chain.

3.3 Accessible Positions

The previous sections gave an overview of how participants in fieldwork felt that migrant women with tertiary education were being essentialised in local labour markets. The following section examines what specific positions are perceived by participants as being accessible for these women.

Accessing Feminised and Racialised Sectors

In line with the literature (Kofman & Raghuram, 2015), it appeared that both Alsace and Veneto stakeholders considered that migrant women tended to find employment in jobs with low social recognition that involved social reproduction, such as cleaners and in-home caregivers. Compared to other economic sectors, migrant women with tertiary education also perceived that they could more easily access employment that related to social reproduction in a broader sense. For instance, social work was also perceived by migrant women as being of more easy reach compared to other jobs. In this regard, De Rudder and Vourc'h (2006: 182) have stressed that in France there has been a racialisation of these positions, connected to the assumption that there is an "ethnic-cultural closeness" with the audience targeted by social policies. Other scholars have also highlighted that these posts tend to be feminised (Kofman & Raghuram, 2015). Consequently, migrant women might more easily access these jobs, although they might simultaneously be confined in a sector that does not necessarily value their background.

In Alsace, both recruiters and graduate migrant women felt that social work was one of the few fields in which migrant women had chances to get an intermediary or graduate job. For instance, Drake, a recruiter in Alsace, found that the sector was "very open". Similarly, Clemensia, who was born in Senegal and was looking for employment in France, felt that social work was accessible to migrant women.

> *[In] all social stuff [jobs], in general, there is always a cultural diversity. Not only* énarques,[3] *let's say, nor good whites with blue eyes. So, in general, these are middle-class, let's say, rather open-minded. And yeah, when you work in the social sector, in general, you are open-minded, yeah.* (Clemensia, born in Senegal, unemployed, France).

In Veneto, graduate migrant women also mentioned jobs related to social work as being obtainable, especially if they wanted to work as a cultural mediator. These jobs are connected to candidates' migrant identity (Liversage, 2009), as they involve speaking in a foreign language, different from the local one. In this regard, Rosanna, who was born in Cameroon, indicated that "many" of her graduate friends were working

[3] Clemensia refers to graduates from the French elite *Ecole Nationale de l'Administration (ENA)*, that trains senior French officials.

with "cooperatives in the field of migrants". However, she highlighted that their jobs did not correspond to their studies. Indeed, working in this field involves that the migrant identity takes precedence over any other skill, ability and aspiration of migrant women's candidates.

Other jobs mentioned as being reachable for migrant women with tertiary education did not directly involve social reproduction but were still connected to their migrants' identity. For instance, in Veneto participants that were Russian speakers considered that posts as export managers that requested speaking Russian were within easy reach. Access to these jobs will be further developed in Chap. 4.

As mentioned, in France graduate women from European non-EU countries who were struggling to find employment in the Alsatian labour markets perceived jobs in international organisations as being more accessible and more in line with their background. These were posts that also partly connected to their migrant identity, as they could put forward their ability to speak *foreign* languages and their multicultural background. However, access to these institutions was limited to candidates that hold the citizenship of one of the member states. As a result, Eastern Europeans could eventually apply to these positions,[4] while access was more limited for women born in countries of Sub-Saharan Africa, as they could access these jobs only once they had acquired the citizenship of a member state.

For instance, faced with a local labour market that appeared to be closed toward foreigners, both Amapola and Azalea, who were respectively born in Albania and Russia, decided to look for opportunities within these institutions. Azalea started as an intern and Amapola as a temporary worker. At the time of the interview, they were both working for an international organisation with permanent contracts as administrative assistants. Although they enjoyed the environment in which they worked, both Azalea and Amapola felt they were overqualified for the job they were doing.

[4] For instance, when research was conducted, the Council of Europe comprised 47 Member states, including Russia, Albania, Ukraine and other European countries outside of the EU. For more details, see: https://www.coe.int

The human resources department of their organisation was also aware of the over-qualification of non-EU women who worked as assistants. Elm, a recruiter at Azalea's and Amapola's international organisation, noticed that there had been a growing number of female candidates from Eastern European countries, who had a high level of education and were applying for intermediary positions.

> *There are many [female candidates] who are highly qualified. When I say very qualified, it also involves people who apply for secretarial competitions [...]. So there is a high level of diploma and sometimes for applications at a much lower level. [...] Some people come into the back door and want to go straight to the big door. And that can generate frustrations, it can generate conflicts in the teams, all these problems must be taken into account.* (Elm, recruiter, France)

A Useful Essentialised Otherness

Scholars have stressed that migrants might be perceived as a useful workforce from the employers' perspective (Castles & Miller, 2009). The precariousness of their administrative status and their positioning in the labour market enables employers to hire them at a lower cost compared to privileged locals (Terray, 2008). Moreover, Tsing (2009) argues that migrants' *difference* has a constitutive role in supply chain capitalism. According to her theory, through subcontracting, employers at the top of the chain can cut labour costs and curb workers' claims, without endorsing any responsibility. Migrants would be mainly employed by the service providers, meaning along the supply chain, and rarely directly at the top of it. The phenomenon has also been highlighted in the Italian food industry (Piro & Sacchetto, 2021).

Interestingly, my fieldwork stressed that this process of outsourcing to migrants' workforce does not exclusively concern jobs at the bottom of the employment structure but also regards graduate positions. Rosamel experience is enlightening in this regard. She was born in Cameroon and moved to Italy to study physiotherapy. After graduating, Rosamel mainly worked for NGOs and cooperatives. As positions in public hospitals continued to be closed to foreigners, Rosamel explained that foreign medical professionals were mostly hired through subcontracting cooperatives, which offered worse working conditions compared to those experienced by Italians directly hired by public institutions. As workers employed through cooperatives were paid less, the system could offer a service that was open every single day of the year, including over Christmas. Rosamel added that, when an Italian went on holiday, the replacement position was guaranteed to be a foreigner: "those with no families", those "who do not worry about going on vacation or not".

> *From the perspective of statistics and service offered, this is excellent: you provide service on Christmas day! But this is because there is a foreigner who works Because you will rarely see an Italian working on the 25th unless they work at the hospital, with shifts and therefore they know that on the 25th the shifts are overpaid. Instead, in cooperatives on the 25th, it is the same salary.* (Rosamel, born in Cameroon, physiotherapist, Italy).

Rosamel's comment echoes that of Castles and Miller (2009): through migration policies and new employment forms characterised by subcontracting, temporary work, and casualisation, migrants continue to be transformed into a "subordinate, flexible labour force" (Ibid: 234). We could add that migrants' flexibility and precariousness enable employers to maintain a system, reducing costs and services which are "excellent", as Rosamel stresses, and open all year long. Moreover, Rosamel's observations stress that welfare services such as health care are also involved in supply chain capitalism (Tsing, 2009).

In addition to the trend introduced above, other recruitment and selection practices aim at benefiting from migrants' essentialised otherness. In this regard, the comments of Shamrock and Sequoia were enlightening. They both worked for the HR department of companies based in Veneto. When talking about the possibility of hiring a migrant candidate, we already stressed that Shamrock pointed out that migrant candidates were carriers of diversity and were therefore evaluated as the bearers of an intrinsic difference, which could be perceived as beneficial or disadvantageous for the company. Similarly, Sequoia also perceived migrants as carers of diversity and stressed that, when recruiting, he valued to which extent it was useful to bring this otherness into the company. His remark pushes us to think that migrants' essentialised otherness—in terms of experience, culture and perception of work- is a selection criterion.

> *It is always good to consider the opportunity to possibly include persons who also bring a breath of fresh air, no, different experiences, cultures, ways of understanding work.* (Sequoia, recruiter, Italy).

Similar comments were made in Alsace, in the context of *diversity* management. Daphne, a social worker in a public institution, explained that in the context of diversity management, companies could find it useful to hire workers that corresponded to the diversity of their clients. As a result, candidates were also hired because they were perceived as intrinsically different from an imaginary representation of the white majority.

> *If I want to correspond to the image of my customers, from a marketing point of view, I hire different people, Asians, Blacks. That's it. But for the quota of diversity, exoticism, they will favour women. But it will not necessarily be for executive positions, be careful. For* cadres,[5] *it's quite a bit more difficult. It opens a little, I don't say that it doesn't... Let's say that Sub-Saharans are preferred when they play football.* (Daphne, social worker, France).

In the context of diversity management, Daphne found that "diverse" women, and especially Black women, would be preferred over men, although they would not be hired for managerial positions (*cadre*). This trend relates to the eroticisation of migrant women's bodies, which will be further analysed in Chap. 4.

3.4 The Variable Geometry of Stratifications

The previous sections described how local labour markets are stratified in terms of gender, racialisation, and class. It should be emphasised that these stratifications and essentialism in the recruitment and selection

[5] *Cadre* is a category with blurred boundaries that includes both workers who use in-depth knowledge to perform their job and managers with supervisory functions (Hamiot & Merle, 2017).

process are not applied in the same way all along the employment structure. They might change according to the characteristics of the employing structure, and depending on recruiters' and social workers' practices.

Diversified Employers

The previous section highlighted that stakeholders felt that specific positions in the labour market were more accessible to migrant women. These positions were mainly those feminised that involved social reproduction, would it be in the care, cleaning, health, or eventually social sectors. Besides sectors, stakeholders in Alsace and Veneto distinguished accessibility to jobs based on the specific characteristics of the employing structure. In this regard, Sorrel, who worked as an intermediary recruiter in Veneto, felt that it was difficult to make any "general" considerations. "Each company, each referent", he said, "has its own culture of reference". Despite each company having a specific way of recruiting, converging comments emerged from both fieldworks.

Both in France and Italy, the size of the company appeared as a critical issue. For instance, small and medium companies, especially in the Veneto region, were perceived as more inclined to use essentialist criteria in their selection processes. Recruiters working both for intermediary agencies and directly in HR departments described these businesses in Italy as *padronale*. The adjective alludes to the idea that the enterprises, and by extension, the recruitment and selection process, are exclusively managed by the owner (*padrone*).

Conversely, recruiters both in Italy and France had the feeling that larger companies would be less discerning on the gender, racialisation, and country of birth of candidates. In Veneto, Sycamore, a recruiter for a multinational company, highlighted that his enterprise had adopted specific policies for an equal balance between gender within the teams. As a result, Sycamore, who was looking at that time for an engineer, indicated that being a woman could be an advantage in this specific recruitment and selection process.

In Alsace, Dianella also worked as a recruiter for a multinational company and shared the same feelings as Sycamore. Moreover, she indicated that her company wanted to increase the internationalisation of its staff. As a result, top management wanted to attract "talented" workers with multicultural backgrounds. Nonetheless, Dianella noted that there was a contrast between the direction's policies and the attitude of "front-line managers", who were reluctant to welcome migrant workers into their teams.

> *We are in a company that increasingly wants to internationalise. So, I have field managers who are going to be a bit reluctant, and, on the other side, I have the political discourse and the top management who are going to be more [inclined to] attract talent, of people who have multicultural backgrounds [...]. So, as I am on a production site, I have very hands-on managers... very locals. Quite often, I mean, they're still going to be a little out of step with that kind of position. But since they know they can't tell me [what they think], they will invent excuses.* (Dianella, recruiter, France).

The previous observations that emerged from the field echo existing literature that sees the size of companies as a crucial variable for understanding the strategies and logic of recruitment and selection (Fullin, 2016). According to these publications, there would be a lower rate of discrimination by the medium-large companies, whose more standardised procedures would enable foreign/migrant candidates not to be rejected at the first contact. This positive description of large-sized enterprises is nuanced by Kmec (2006). The scholar estimates that in the absence of control and monitoring procedures, the formal recruitment and selection procedures do not guarantee out-group hiring—namely the recruitment and selection of candidates who are perceived as belonging to other groups in terms of gender and racialisation.

The analysis based on the empirical data collected for the book adds to this literature. On the one hand, it stresses that within the same large company, there can be tensions and contradictory behaviours according to the levels of management. Top-management might officially declare its openness towards migrant workers, while medium and low-level managers can be reluctant to include these workers in their teams. Moreover, interaction with research participants invites one to be particularly attentive to the specific positions to which "diversity", especially that of (eventually essentialised) graduate migrant women, provides access. Indeed, researchers need to examine whether these women have equal access to any job, including that of top managers, or if they are confined to feminine positions that aim at favouring the marketing image of the company towards its customers.

In addition to the size of the company, another critical characteristic that deserves our attention concerns the position of the employer company along the supply chain. In this regard, relevant observations were made by Carmel and Rosamel. Carmel was born in Nigeria and used to work as a bilingual administrative assistant in Alsace. She told me that when she was looking for employment in the area, it was mainly in intermediary agencies where she felt judged for the colour of her skin. On the other hand, Rosamel, who was born in Cameroon and worked as a physiotherapist in Veneto, mentioned that during her job hunting, she mainly felt disdained by the employees of subcontracting cooperatives. From her viewpoint, their rude attitude was paradoxical as these structures mostly relied on migrants' work.

> *It was more in [subcontracting] cooperatives where I felt this contempt, which is a strange thing because 80% of cooperatives only [hire] foreigners. […] And therefore a cooperative in my opinion should welcome foreigners differently, I don't say give them crowns, but its workforce is foreigners, 80% [of the workers] certainly [are]. The cooperative where I did substitutions [to cover] emergencies, it was because Italians would go on vacation, in line with their contracts […] but whoever covered, who replaced [them] was a foreigner, who had no family, who didn't bother to go on holiday or not.* (Rosamel, born in Cameroon, physiotherapist, Italy).

Although this trend seemed paradoxical to Rosamel, it fits Tsing (2009)'s analysis of supply chains. Tsing (2009) precisely highlights that supply chain capitalism is based on inequalities according to gender, class, and racialisation. It is through the use of diversity and inequalities that labour costs can be cut and workers' claims refrained, while top-of-the-chain is released from all responsibility for labour.

Recruiters' Levers

After emphasising the differences in recruitment and selection practices according to the size of the company and its position in the supply-chain line, the following section focuses on the individual recruiter's *agency*. To which extent do recruiters feel that they can freely choose a candidate?

Whether they worked in an HR department or for an intermediary agency, recruiters in fieldwork described their job as being primarily that of an intermediary. While recruiters employed by agencies indicated that they worked for clients, those working for private companies stressed that their job depended on managers' or team leaders' decisions. For instance, Dianella, who worked for an HR department in Alsace, emphasised that her choices depended on the field managers for whom she worked. "As an HR [employee], I am a support service", she found, "so I'm going to help managers look for the right profiles".

Recruiters appeared as not being alone in the decision-making of recruiting and selecting a candidate. Nonetheless, they had different perceptions of their margin of action in the recruitment and selection process. While some felt that their job consisted of complying with the wishes of clients or managers, others indicated that they could influence the outcome and even change the mind of future employers. Scheme 3.3 summarises recruiters' perception of their agency in the recruitment and selection process.

At the first extreme of the continuum is Sirelli, who worked as a recruiter in Veneto. From her perspective, working as a recruiter in an intermediary agency implied "completely giving way" to her clients'

Scheme 3.3 Recruiters' perception of their agency in the recruitment and selection process

• Recruiters need to comply with all clients' and managers' requests (including essentialist criteria)	• Recruiters can influence the recruitment and selection process and present candidates that do not correspond to clients' and managers' essentialist criteria

wishes. As a result, Sirelli found that recruiters should please clients in "everything", which included requirements connected to gender, racialisation, and class of the candidates.

> *Let's say that what an [employment] agency does in general, not only an intermediary agency but also an agency that offers other types of services, such as the [communication agency] where I am now, is trying to completely give way to the clients' [wishes] and therefore to satisfy them in everything and for everything, that is, when a prestigious customer makes all kinds of requests, we must try to exhaust them, end of discussion.* (Sirelli, recruiter, Italy).

On the other extreme of the continuum when compared to Sirelli, some recruiters found they could influence the outcome. While Sirelli seemed not to question clients' "all kinds of requests", Sorrel, who also worked as a recruiter in Veneto, believed that he could present a person whose gender, nationality, skin colour or look did not match the initial request of the client. Sorrel gave the example of a specific recruitment and selection process he followed, in which the employer wanted to hire a man. The future worker was expected to operate in a foundry, in a male-dominated team. Sorrel explained that he interviewed a woman that did not have a graduate degree but had previously trained, and had a long-lasting experience. The recruiter decided to present the candidate to the company, which rejected her at first, but Sorrel insisted.

> *I decided to present her to the company that immediately discarded her on paper, telling me "No, she is not good", tried to turn it around for a moment, and I said "fine, let's give her an opportunity, you should see her, I liked her, just see her, and then we can talk about it". Indeed, he chose her.* (Sorrel, recruiter, Italy).

As a consequence of Sorrel's insistence, the client changed his mind and accepted hiring a candidate that did not correspond to the gender expected. "It is also nice sometimes", said Sorrel, "to be able to make people change ideas". This example illustrates that recruiters might influence the selection process and facilitate or refrain specific candidates from accessing jobs.

Similarly in Alsace, Dianella, an HR in a private company, also thought she could influence the outcome of the selection process. Dianella indicated that she often had to negotiate with field managers, who could have a priori bias towards migrant women. However, Dianella told me that she was delighted as she had recently managed to hire a migrant woman for a technical position.

> *We are in a region where there is a particular form of - how do you say - fear and almost racism, with possible discrimination against people [...]. And for specific origins, well, I think managers can invent pretexts and they might not always be open-minded. [...] To this day, I have no regrets at all for hiring [the Colombian graduate]. Indeed, I hired a woman of foreign origins for a production position, so it was a technical position. I am pleased with myself: a young woman with little experience.* (Dianella, recruiter, France)

Social Workers' Orientation

Both in France and Italy, social workers tended to acknowledge that migrant women were struggling to see their educational qualifications recognised. Nonetheless, their practice in supporting migrant women mainly gave priority to accessing employment, whatever it was, regardless of the women's previous experience. As a result, graduate migrant women tended to be orientated towards feminised and racialised positions at the bottom of the employment structure, namely in the care and cleaning services.

Daphne, who worked in Alsace for a public institution that followed unemployed persons, described the trajectories of graduate migrant women with whom she had interacted. Daphne stressed that, when doable, she tried to support these women so that they found employment in their fields. "They have already lost a lot", she felt, "if they can keep their professional identity, it's better for them". However, she indicated that most of the graduates she followed had to "restart from scratch". Daphne mentioned a specific graduate woman who had managed to find employment in line with her studies, but she specified that it was because the woman was "resourceful" (*débrouillarde*) that she had managed to do so: the woman learned French and found internships by herself. Daphne's comment suggests that despite counting on social workers' support, finding employment in one's field falls mainly on migrant women's shoulders.

> *Our role is to try to [help them to] learn French following courses while in apprenticeship for a job. It's what we call vocational training. […] [Migrant women] integrate training courses. This means that, once they speak French, they can join a cooking course,* cuisine actuelle, *or things like that. And, also, as a maternal assistant too, mostly in these areas.* (Daphne, social worker, France).

From migrant women's perspective, I mentioned that Cassia, who was born in Senegal and lived in France, had quite a bitter experience when interacting with public institutions. Cassia, who worked for over six years as an administrative assistant in Dakar, was especially critical towards the social worker that followed her case at Pôle Emploi, the French agency in charge of providing support to unemployed workers. As mentioned, Cassia felt that her counsellor only reacted to her emails when she asked to enrol in training for care jobs, at the bottom of the employment structure. Conversely, Cassia indicated that he did not reply when she looked for training opportunities more in line with her previous employment.

Like in Alsace, social workers in Veneto also indicated that one of the main objectives of the support provided to migrants was to find any employment, regardless of the person's background. In this regard, Selena, a social worker, mentioned that she still tried to take migrant women's backgrounds into account but the path towards the recognition of diplomas was so complicated and costly that she had to direct them towards less qualifying training.

> *[On her CV], Giorgia*[6] *had written 'nurse' […] at the Hospital of T. in Ghana. And she wrote it [in her CV] because indeed, these are skills. And indeed, I would like her to follow a training course for care assistants, for instance. Because the path to be a nurse is too complicated, and [at the NGO] we don't have the funding to finance three years of [nurse] training course. A training*

[6] The name has been changed to protect privacy.

course for care assistants is more accessible for us to pay for, and maybe it is not that far [from being a nurse]. [...] I wanted to make her diploma recognised because in Ghana she was a nurse, but it is an uphill journey, we did not manage. (Selena, social worker, Italy).

Both in France and Italy, social workers emphasised the importance of training. Language training, in particular, was perceived as a fundamental first step to facilitate access to employment. Successively, graduate migrant women could be directed towards professional training that in both regions mainly focused on reproductive jobs, such as cleaning, caring, and eventually cooking. In this regard, Scrinzi (2013) has highlighted how these training programmes might contribute to the construction of "non-qualification" and racialisation. Although social workers perceived these courses as facilitating access to employment, they also contributed to confining migrant women in feminised and racialised positions at the bottom of the employment structure.

* * *

The chapter has highlighted how the different actors involved in the process of accessing employment, namely recruiters, social workers and migrant women candidates, perceive stratifications of the labour market and the impact of essentialism in accessing jobs. Despite differences between France and Italy, it appeared that in both contexts there are complex employment stratifications and essentialist representations of migrant women based on gender, racialisation, and class influence their access to jobs.

The chapter also identified some of the working positions that are perceived as being more accessible for migrant women and that tend to correspond to feminised and racialised jobs, such as those in the care and social work sectors. In parallel, it emerged that employers also benefit from the essentialised otherness of migrant women, especially in the context of supply chain capitalism and diversity management. The chapter also stressed that the impact of essentialism in recruitment and selection might vary according to companies' size and their position in the supply chain.

Finally, the analysis emphasised the *agency* of recruiters and social workers, stressing that through their practices, they might reproduce or challenge essentialism and employment stratifications. The following chapter will analyse more in detail how essentialism influences the recruitment and selection of candidates, by focusing on the assessment of skills.

References

Ambrosini, M. (2009). Migrazioni, territori, appartenenze: una relazione contrastata. In B. Ghiringhelli & S. Marelli (Eds.), *Accogliere gli immigrati. Testimonianze di inclusione socio-economicati* (pp. 55–75). Carocci.

Amelina, A., & Horvath, K. (2020). Regimes of intersection: Facing the manifold interplays of discourses, institutions, and inequalities in the regulation of migration. *Migration Letters, 17*(4), 487–497.

Bourdieu, P. (1986). The forms of capital. In J. Richardson (Ed.), *Handbook of theory and research for the sociology of education* (pp. 241–258). Greenwood.

Castles, S., & Miller, M. J. (2009). *The age of migration: International population movements in the modern world*. Palgrave Macmillan.

De Rudder, V., & Vourc'h, F. (2006). Les discriminations racistes dans le monde du travail. In D. Fassin & E. Fassin (Eds.), *De la question sociale à la question raciale ? Représenter la société française*. La Découverte.

Fassin, D. (2006). Du déni à la dénégation. Psychologie politique de la représentation des discriminations. In D. Fassin & E. Fassin (Eds.), *De la question sociale à la question raciale? Représenter la société française* (pp. 133–157). La Découverte.

Fullin, G. (2016). Labour market outcomes of immigrants in a south European country: Do race and religion matter? *Work, Employment and Society, 30*(3), 391–409.

Hamiot, J.-Y., & Merle, K. (2017). La représentation sociale de carrière de cadres face à la mondialisation des médias. *Question (s) de Management, 4*, 91–100.

Kmec, J. A. (2006). White hiring agent's orgnizational practices and out-group hiring. *Social Science Research, 35*, 668–701.

Kofman, E., & Raghuram, P. (2015). *Gendered migrations and global social reproduction*. Palgrave Macmillan UK.

Liversage, A. (2009). Vital conjunctures, shifting horizons: High-skilled female immigrants looking for work. *Work, Employment & Society, 23*(1), 120–141.
Piro, V., & Sacchetto, D. (2021). Subcontracted racial capitalism: The interrelationship of race and production in meat processing plants. *Work in the Global Economy, 1*(1–2), 33–53.
Scrinzi, F. (2013). *Genre, migrations et emplois domestiques en France et en Italie. Construction de la non-qualification et de l'altérité ethnique*. Pétra.
Terray, E. (2008). Pourquoi partent-ils? In C. Rodier & E. Terray (Eds.), *Immigration: fantasmes et réalités. Pour une alternative à la fermeture des frontières*. La Découverte.
Tsing, A. (2009). Supply chains and the human condition. *Rethinking Marxism, 21*(2), 148–176.

4

"She Wanted me to Take a Dictation Exercise". Essentialism and the Embodiment of Skills

Callaia was born in Niger, where she worked for over ten years as a midwife. By the beginning of the 1990s, she moved to Alsace following her French partner who she met in Niger. As she wanted to continue working in her field, Callaia looked for information regarding how she could get her education and experience recognised in France. After a long process, she was informed that her Nigerien degree would not enable her to work as a midwife in France. She could work instead as a nursing assistant in maternity. Callaia wondered if she should enrol in training once again. She went to a midwives' school to learn about the enrollment procedure. However, she was faced with an unpleasant surprise that curbed her desire to register. Being born in a former French colony, in which one of the official languages is that of the former coloniser, Callaia had pursued all her studies in French. However, when arriving at the midwives' school, the director of the institution indicated that she wanted her to take a dictation exercise to see if she could read and write in French.

> *So, I went to [the midwife] school to [get informed]. It was very humiliating because there was the school principal who wanted me to take a dictation exercise to see if I could read and write in French.* (Callaia, nurse, France).

A.-I. Romens, *Deconstructing Essentialism*,
https://doi.org/10.1007/978-3-031-14399-1_4

After this episode, Callaia decided not to enrol at the midwives' school and started working as a nurse assistant at a hospital maternity service. After nearly nine years of working as a nurse assistant, Callaia decided to take an exam to enter a nursing school and succeeded. When I met her, she had been working as a nurse for over eleven years. Callaia's story illustrates that skills, including language skills, are not external assets which are objectively scrutinised but they are embodied (Wolkowitz, 2006). As a result, skills might be valued or disregarded according to scrutinisers' essentialist representations.

This chapter analyses in detail how knowledge, know-how, capacities, and skills are embodied and assessed depending on who holds them. More specifically, the chapter proposes to identify and deconstruct essentialist criteria in the recruitment and selection process, by focusing on the assessment of education, experience, language and soft skills.

4.1 Embodiment in the Recruitment and Selection Process

The Social Construction of Migrant Women's Bodies

Scholars have argued that the body is not limited to its physicality. It is also socially constructed and embedded in gender, class, and racial relations (Foucault, 1991). Sociologists have analysed the nexus between body and paid work, from multiple perspectives. For instance, Wolkowitz (2006: 175) highlights that gender, racial and class ideologies play a significant role in "naturalising aspects of bodily capacities". Moreover, she stresses that the capitalist labour process decides which capacities are to be *recognised* and *recompensed* and which are *normalised*, using gender, racialisation, and class as a justification (Ibid: 175). Wolkowitz highlights that these ideologies might hide the efforts that workers put into performing their roles. The scholar gives the example of migrant women that work in the domestic sector. From her perspective, employment of migrant women in these jobs partly relies on *naturalising* migrant women's ability to care, based on "racialised imagined differences, between employers and their servant" (Ibid:161). Similar inputs are provided by Scrinzi (2013) in her study on the recruitment and selection of domestic workers in Italy and France. The scholar highlights that in both contexts, there are processes of essentialism of migrant women. In Italy, Scrinzi (2013) observes that recruitment and selection of domestic workers are based on essentialism that associates specific "races" and "cultures of origin" with skills related to domestic and care work.

Most of the literature that studies the relationship between body and labour has focused on *bodywork*, which includes service sector employees who work with their bodies and the bodies of others (McDowell, 2011). Wolkowitz (2006) suggests going beyond these types of jobs and studying embodied beings in all research regarding employment. From her perspective, embodiment needs to be also studied "when it is not explicitly targeted by the employer or mentioned by the informant as such" (Ibid: 182). In order to include Wolkowitz's invitation, the chapter studies how the embodiment of migrant women's skills interferes with their assessment by recruiters, and conversely, what expectations recruiters have concerning migrant women's bodily capacities, covering sectors that go beyond the traditional focus on bodywork.

Subjectivity in the Recruitment and Selection Process

In my fieldwork, both in France and Italy, recruiters referred to the subjectivity that is involved in the selection process. In this regard, Sirelli, a recruiter in Veneto, indicated that "selection is not a science" and highlighted how subjectivity interfered in her way of assessing candidates' abilities.

> *[It relates] a bit to intuition, because in the end, I think that this [intuition] matters a lot in the selection process. [...] Selection is not a science. What matters a lot is the nature of the meeting between the person who selects and the person who is being selected; what matters is the feeling that arouses.* (Sirelli, recruiter, Italy).

In France, Dianella, a recruiter, also stressed the role of subjectivity and feelings. She described recruitment and selection processes as a moment of "mutual seduction", in which it was very difficult to get a "real idea" of the person.

> *It is a moment of mutual seduction, where the company will say what it wants to say, and often, [it] sells a position from a very good angle, very beautiful angle... and then, well, the candidate is also always showing himself in his best light, and I find it extremely easy for smart candidates - and we always have smart candidates-, it's often very easy to fool the recruiter.* (Dianella, recruiter, France).

Drake, a recruiter in France, methodologically described the criteria he used to select candidates. He indicated he based his decision on a tryptic composed of skills, motivation, and potential. The recruiter stressed that skills included knowledge, know-how, but also the "know how to be" (*savoir être*), which he connected to behaviour. We can wonder to what extent his preconceptions interfered in assessing this *savoir être*. The question will be further explored when analysing the assessment of soft skills.

Shamrock, a recruiter in Italy, also gave details on how he selected candidates. Shamrock indicated that he distinguished "more technical" profiles, which involved specific technical skills, from positions for which soft, human, and interpersonal skills were needed, like in the case of managers. For selecting the former profiles, Shamrock focused on knowledge, education and experience, while for the latter, assessment involved more subjective criteria which will be developed further in the following sections.

In both regions, the most experienced recruiters described the ongoing transformations in their jobs and more specifically referred to how the criteria used to recruit and select candidates have changed. Both Dianella in France and Saffron in Italy observed a shift from an attitude deemed more *passive* in which recruiters were waiting for applications, towards a more *active* position where candidates were sought directly within competing companies. In Dianella's view, the use of new techniques related to *headhunting* had the effect of widening the inequalities in accessing graduate employment. On the one hand, those who were already working were contacted by headhunters and could therefore improve their working conditions. On the other hand, outsiders, such as migrant women with tertiary education, had fewer opportunities. According to Dianella's observation, being unemployed or employed in lower positions had almost become an unsurpassable obstacle to accessing graduate jobs.

> *The companies will all be looking for more or less the same thing in the future and the same skills. So you have to attract talent. And so, it will change the way of recruiting [...]. We will be more in a proactive role and in a dynamic search for talents, than waiting gently for the [cover] letter, the spontaneous application [of candidates] that they are willing to send us. I think there was perhaps a greater passivity in the past, when there were [many] candidates. [...] Now, there is still mass unemployment, but it concerns specific populations that nobody wants [to hire] in the end. I know, it's ugly to say, but it's true.* (Dianella, recruiter, France)

4.2 Assessing Embodied Skills

In the previous section, recruiters indicated that assessing candidates' suitability for a job involved scrutinising education and experience, as well as communication and soft skills. In this section, I analyse the impact that essentialism based on gender, class and racialisation and influenced by colonial legacy and global inequalities has in the process of assessing these skills.

The Global Hierarchy of Foreign Education

Different theories have been developed to explain the "educational mismatch" of migrant workers, namely the fact they tend to find employment in jobs that do not value their educational background. According to *human capital theory,* migrants have difficulties in transferring their titles due to the institutional distance between the country where they have obtained their education and the country of immigration (Chiswick & Miller, 2009). A critical limitation of this literature is that it does not take into account gender, racialisation, and class relations. In this regard,

Kofman (2012) stresses that knowledge associated with feminised reproductive sectors of the labour market tends to be overlooked, while *embrained* knowledge which tends to be used in male-dominated sectors has an easier transferability.

The challenge of having education recognised was stressed by participants in my French and Italian fieldwork, especially by migrant women with tertiary education. For instance, Abelia, who graduated in Russia, mentioned her shock when she understood that her diploma was not as valued as she thought it would be.

> *I had to validate my Russian diplomas. [...] I thought that I had a great diploma and, here, in France, the super diploma did not represent a large-thing. That's a bit of a shame.* (Abelia, born in Russia, Librarian, France).

In France, social workers also emphasised that migrant women struggled to see their diplomas recognised. For instance, Dalia, a social worker in an Alsatian NGO, found that this was the main obstacle that migrant women with tertiary education faced when trying to access graduate employment. Dalia underlined that there was a lack of specific procedures to facilitate the recognition of foreign diplomas or degree titles. She explained that, together with her colleagues, she was using the official French platform ENIC-NARIC to validate titles but foreign degrees were "very, but very, very rarely recognised". Dalia referred to a woman she knew who used to work as a dentist in Georgia, but whose education had not been validated in France.

> *Her dentistry diploma, which she passed in Georgia, [was] not at all valid in France. So, [at the NGO] we do diploma translations to see if ever people want to take up a level of study, on the ENIC-NARIC platform. We can do translations and validate the level they have obtained. But foreign diplomas are very, but very, very rarely recognised in fact in France.* (Dalia, social worker, France).

In Italy, migrant women also identified the lack of recognition of education gained abroad as one of the main challenges they had faced to access graduate employment. From the recruiters' perspective, Senna, a recruiter in Veneto, indicated that it was extremely challenging for her to assess education gained abroad. Senna specifically indicated that education gained in Africa and Eastern Europe was not perceived as having "the same level of quality".

> *Maybe degrees abroad in countries I don't know like... Africa or Eastern Europe, they may not be seen as, with the same level of quality [...]. People turn up their noses, let's say, if we ask: 'Where did you graduate?', 'In Nigeria'. Who knows what training is offered there; who knows what kind of doctor you can be?* (Senna, recruiter, Italy).

Senna's comment could be mindful of the *screening hypothesis theory*, as schooling abroad has an unclear meaning for her (Chiswick & Miller, 2009). According to the theory, the tendency to exclude candidates would be "more prevalent" for migrants who studied in countries with "labour markets and institutions distant from the destination countries" (Ibid: 164). However, we can wonder to what extent Alsatian and Veneto degrees are worth more than that of African or Eastern European universities, and whether Senna would have made the same comment about qualifications obtained in countries of the Global North.

In this regard, an interesting insight comes from the analysis of global university rankings. Scholars have argued that these rankings reinforce the "Western hegemony" in higher education (Lo, 2011). Despite this bias, it is interesting to note that according to the THE—Times Higher Education World University Rankings—two of Veneto's and Alsace's main universities are rated below several African universities. For instance, the university of Ca' Foscari in Venice, has a lower score than four universities in South Africa, one in Uganda, and ranks at the same level as the Covenant University and the University of Ibadan in Nigeria, while the University of Haute Alsace, which is Alsace second main university, ranks significantly lower.[1] As a result, despite indexes, titles gained abroad seemed to be rather assessed according to representations based on global hierarchies inherited from the colonial past (Grosfoguel et al., 2015), leading to a stratification of diplomas that reflected global inequalities.

---

[1] THE, Times Higher Education World University Rankings: https://www.timeshighereducation.com/world-university-rankings/2019/world-ranking

In this regard, Selena, a social worker at an Italian NGO, estimated that foreign degrees were evaluated differently depending on the position in the international arena of the country in which they were obtained. For instance, a degree obtained in the UK would be preferred, compared to one from Nigeria.

> *The difficulty is to transform [migrant women's] qualifications so that they are recognized here [in Italy]. To tell you the truth, it is practically impossible [...]. It also depends on where you have obtained the degree because, obviously, if you have a degree from London, it changes, right... Unfortunately, that's how it is.* (Selena, social worker, Italy)

Assessing Experience Gained Abroad

Together with education, experience is also used as a filter to assess skills. Overall, it appeared that in both research contexts, migrant women's experiences gained abroad tended to be disregarded. In France, Daphne, a social worker, found that recruiters tended to focus only on the experience gained locally. To illustrate her point, she imitated a conversation between a recruiter and a migrant candidate with experience abroad.

> *Because we do not value the skills acquired abroad. [...] Often, if you [a migrant candidate] arrive, [the recruiters] will ask you: "What working experience do you have?"; "Well I was - I don't know what - abroad"; "No, no, but in France". But no, the person must be taken as a whole.* (Daphne, social worker, France).

Echoing Daphne's comment, most migrant women in Alsace indicated that they felt their experience abroad was undervalued in the selection process, especially when it was gained in countries considered as being peripheral (Grosfoguel et al., 2015). For instance, this was the feeling of Acacia, who was born in Moldova and trained both in her country of birth and in France. Before moving to Alsace, Acacia had worked in Moldova as a teacher of literature, an editor, and a radio broadcaster. When applying for being a leader at a community centre in Alsace, Acacia felt that, although she had relevant working experience in Moldova, it was mainly her short experience in France that was taken into consideration.

> *I tried to highlight the experiences and studies I did here. Because I know that, it's more important from the point of view of employers here. But I do not want to say that all I have lived elsewhere has to be cancelled, [or] that it's not important. It's important for me but for someone who wants to hire someone, I think it's rather interesting and important what we have done in the French context, here.* (Acacia, born in Moldova, leader at a community centre, France).

Experience abroad was particularly disregarded when gained in countries perceived as weaker in the global hierarchy inherited from the colonial past (Grosfoguel et al., 2015). From the recruiters' perspective, a striking example was given by Saffron, who worked as an intermediary recruiter for more than twenty years in Veneto. When I met him, I knew from online research before the interview that Saffron's agency was looking for export managers that were fluent in English. By the end of the interview, I hypothesised the profile of a woman candidate that would be born in Ghana and had experience in export management in that country. I asked Saffron to comment whether he would hire her for a position his agency was currently advertising to trade shocking freezers abroad. Saffron's reaction to my suggestion highlights how representations based on colonial legacy and global inequalities influence the assessment of the professional experience. The perception that Saffron had of African economies appeared to have a significant influence on the way he valued, or more probably underestimated, experience gained in that geographical area.

> *A Ghanaian, who sold, I don't know, pots for cooking for explorers, maybe... Export Manager for Western Africa. Here we are talking about Europe. And only Europe. Why? For a straightforward reason, because these products, to be sold outside of Europe, must respond to different characteristics, so if I sell in the United States, if I sell in Canada... These are already two different things. And so since these are shocking freezers, in Western Africa what do you think that they might shock freeze? Surely, there is a narrow interest, so it could be interesting if someone wanted to... I mean, there are global interests in Sub-*

> *Saharan Africa, so Ghana and so on; products that are sold there are those that for us are a bit obsolete or not good because they are growing there, petrol, so the benefit goes to the population.* (Saffron, recruiter, Italy).

Although experience gained abroad tended to be undervalued by recruiters, knowledge and know-how that came out from it were still used at the workplace. Previous experience benefited the employers, although they did not compensate it with any monetary or symbolic recognition. For instance, in France, Acacia, whose experience was mentioned above, indicated that when working with youngsters she was using her former skills as a journalist, as together with them she edited and published a community journal, and they went once to speak at a local radio station. "Knowing a bit the work specificity [...], I [could] prepare them in advance to ask the right questions, to be curious, to know what to look for", she said.

In the Italian context, Rosalie, who was born in the Democratic Republic of Congo, also indicated that she was using the *soft skills* she acquired abroad. Before moving to Italy, Rosalie had studied in the DRC, where she worked for over six years as a laboratory assistant. When I met her, she was working as a care assistant at a retirement home in Veneto.

> *With the experience I had working in Africa, I didn't have those problems to relate to someone, to the [retirement home] guests. [...] I already knew, I know how, these are things I have studied. How you have to present things, the way you ask questions and everything. It is something that I had already practised, working at the hospital.* (Rosalie, born in the DRC, care assistant, Italy).

Both cases, that of Acacia in France, and that of Rosalie in Italy, illustrate the phenomenon of invisibilisation of skills gained through previous experience. In line with the literature, it appeared that they were subject to *brain abuse* (Bauder, 2003), meaning the use of their capacities with no compensation. My fieldwork also stresses that the exploitation of migrant women's capacities goes beyond *embrained knowledge* (Kofman, 2012) as it also includes *abuse* of soft skills and skills connected to emotional labour (Hochschild, 2012).

Embodied Language Skills

I propose to focus now on the influence of essentialism in assessing language skills, which tend to be associated with hard skills (Babić & Slavković, 2011). In line with the literature (Lehtovaara & Jyrkinen, 2021), it emerges from my fieldwork that speaking the local language is perceived as a critical issue for accessing employment. For instance, both in France and Italy, social workers perceived learning the local language as crucial to get a job.

My fieldwork highlighted that speaking the local language is an eligibility criterion, even for positions in which workers will be mainly interacting in another language. For instance, Senna, a recruiter in Italy, gave the example of social media managers. Depending on clients' requests, Senna had hired candidates whose mother tongue was English or Russian, and that were in charge of managing the customers' social media in that language. Although she gave priority to *foreign* languages skills when selecting candidates, Senna indicated that not knowing Italian was problematic, as social media managers were not able to communicate properly with their clients. As a result, having good proficiency in Italian was also an eligibility criterion.

Another critical issue concerned the impact of accent when accessing employment. In this regard, Cuban (2013) has stressed that because of their accent, the language knowledge of migrant women tends to be underestimated by employers. This phenomenon was also highlighted by participants in Italy and France. For instance, in France, Azalea, who was born in Russia and worked as an administrative assistant, found that recruiters had prejudices against candidates who had an accent.

> *Unless you speak perfect French, I think there can be some prejudice against you. [...] They really prefer... even my best friend who is from Romania, he speaks... he speaks French quite well, and he experiences the same problems.* (Azalea, born in Russia, administrative assistant, France).

In addition, my fieldwork highlighted another crucial issue when it comes to local language skills: fluency in the local language did not preclude recruiters from having stereotypes regarding candidates, especially if they were born in former colonies. Indeed, colonialism might have left a common language in the countries of the former empire. As a result, French and Italian can be the mother tongue of migrant women candidates, especially those from former French colonies. This commonality should, at least in theory, be an asset for migrants coming from the former colonial areas. However, interviews in the field lead one to conclude that, although migrant women might be fluent in French, their language skills can still be disregarded. The experience of Callaia that was mentioned in the introduction of the chapter is eloquent from that perspective. The woman was fluent in French, as she was born in a former colony in which French continues to be one of the official languages, but her language skills were questioned by stakeholders in Alsace.

Besides speaking the local language, proficiency in a *foreign* language, different from the local official one, is increasingly becoming a crucial feature in the production process. Scholars estimate that skills in a foreign language are a major factor affecting wage and labour opportunities (Garrouste, 2008). However, Isphording (2013) warns that the returns to foreign language skills might vary across the wage distribution, according to the sector, the language, and the specific position that is accessed. My fieldwork stresses that proficiency in a foreign language is not equally valued depending on who embodies it, and how the candidate is perceived in terms of gender, racialisation, and class.

When it comes to foreign language skills, both in Italy and France, recruiters highlighted that proficiency in English was an asset to access specific positions, such as that of social media manager. In Veneto, Senna, a recruiter who often looked for English-speaking candidates to work as social media managers, indicated that the workers she had hired were mainly from the United Kingdom, and the United States. When I asked her if she ever had candidates from Nigeria, Senna told me that she did but did not consider their applications. From her perspective, Nigerian English, both written and spoken, was not "*sustainable*" for her customers.

> *We did not consider [the Nigerian candidates] because that is a [type of] English that is not sustainable for our customers, both written and spoken; at the spoken level, the accent is very heavy and probably they will also struggle.* (Senna, recruiter, Italy).

In Italy, it appeared that graduates from Sub-Saharan Africa who were fluent in English and French were more likely to see their language skills valued in social work or in jobs that involved interacting with English- or French-speaking African migrants, such as cultural mediators. As mentioned in the previous chapter, scholars estimate that the presence of migrants in this sector is related to the assumption that there is an "ethnic-cultural closeness" with the audience targeted by social policies (De Rudder & Vourc'h, 2006: 182).

Although foreign language skills could facilitate access to social work both in France and Italy, it should be emphasised that these skills also hid the other abilities of migrant women. Access to these working positions might not particularly value migrant women's educational background, as illustrated by Rosanna, who was born in Cameroon and lived in Italy.

> *Many [Africans] are working now with NGOs, many, many. Because they know French, English and Italian and, I don't know, something else. They have the opportunity to work with cooperatives, with migrants. It has nothing to do with what they have studied, but they have found [work].* (Rosanna, born in Cameroon, care assistant, Italy).

In France, my fieldwork suggests that proficiency in English of Black African women was likely to provide access to a broader range of jobs. A relevant experience in this regard was that of Carmel. She was born in Nigeria and studied both in her birth country and in France. Although Carmel indicated that it had happened that she felt judged by the colour of her skin when looking for employment in Alsace, she also stressed that she had managed to access positions that had English as a crucial eligibility criterion and were not related to social work. For instance, she had found employment as a bilingual administrative assistant working first for private companies, and then for international organisations.

Business and international trade services also emerged as a sector in which migrant women could eventually value their foreign language skills, especially when local companies had specific commercial ties with other countries. In this regard, Veneto is one of the Italian regions with the highest value of the export business and countries of the former Soviet Union are among the main areas with which local enterprises trade

(Ufficio Statistica della Regione Veneto, 2018). As a result, companies in Veneto are often looking for Russian-speaking candidates to work in export management.

When it comes to recruitment in the field of export management, it emerged from my fieldwork that the valuing of foreign language skills also varied according to the candidate's country of birth. For instance, Saffron, a recruiter in Veneto, estimated that employers could have specific expectations concerning the nationality of the candidate. For instance, he explained that when looking for candidates that are fluent in Russian, the selection process might provide an advantage to only a subset of the Russian speakers, according to trade relations, country of birth, and representations.

> *Nationality is sometimes specifically requested, for example, for the back office, nationality is asked there, 'I want the Russian and not the Ukrainian', just to be specific, because the Russian is Russian, and the Ukrainian is Ukrainian.* (Saffron, recruiter, Italy).

Despite Saffron's comment, my fieldwork suggested that export management was not completely closed to other Russian-speaking women. For instance, when I met her, Veronica, who was born in Ukraine, had been working in export management for over seven years. She underlined that it was thanks to her Russian language skills that she had had a career in Veneto.

> *For the jobs I was looking for, it didn't influence that much [the fact of being born abroad], because they were looking for a [Russian] native speaker for this job. But if I would be looking for a job, I don't know, for example in the administration of a company that doesn't care about exporting, I don't know if maybe they would prefer, if they would give priority to an Italian. In my opinion, yes.* (Veronica, born in Ukraine, business manager, Italy)

Assessing Soft Skills

Scholars stress that soft skills are becoming crucial within the production processes, although they might refer to "generic human qualities", such as sociability and adaptability, which assessment is highly subjective (Mezzadra & Neilson, 2013: 141). In this regard, the previous chapter highlighted that both in France and Italy recruiters and social workers referred to essentialist beliefs that associated racialisation, class and gender with behaviours and personality traits that were either appreciated or denigrated by employers. For instance, in France Daphne, a social worker, indicated that the elegance, vanity and submissiveness of Chechen women were seen with a favourable eye to access service jobs. Conversely, Daphne found that African women tended to be disregarded because they were seen as having too strong a personality. In the same vein, recruiters in Italy, such as Sirelli and Senecio, made similar comments on women from Eastern European countries, indicating that they could be disregarded for specific positions because they were perceived as being either "authoritative, strong, almost grouchy" and associated with *in-home carers*. These examples stressed how essentialism based on the intersection of class, racialisation and gender influenced the selection process in Italy and France, leading to the exclusion of migrant women.

We propose to deepen the analysis by highlighting that the criteria used by recruiters to assess soft skills can lead to the exclusion of migrant women with tertiary education, including when they do not express specific preferences in terms of gender, nationality or class. To analyse the mechanism, it is necessary to study in detail how recruiters perceive and assess soft skills. Both in Alsace and Veneto, recruiters related soft skills to communication capacities. For example, Shamrock, a recruiter in Italy, indicated that a *good* candidate for a marketing position should demonstrate *excellent* communication skills. Shamrock specified that this criterion included non-verbal and para-verbal communication, and gave details on how he assessed these skills.

> *You can immediately notice it perhaps in the gesturalism of the candidate, in the way in which he puts himself, in the way in which he puts himself even concerning his tone of voice... if he speaks calmly, if he is quiet, if he is tense, if... there is an infinite number then...* (Shamrock, recruiter, Italy).

Dianella, a recruiter in France, indicated that, when looking for managers, she was also concerned about their *courage*. I asked her to explain what she understood with the term.

> *The* courage *[means], well, to say things to collaborators, to know how to say "No" to a collaborator; to know how to say to a collaborator "This year I did not put you up for a pay raise, because you did not deserve it". And not to say "Well, I did not put you up for a pay raise, because I had no budget".* (Dianella, recruiter, France).

The criteria mentioned by recruiters in Alsace and Veneto involve a high level of scrutiny over candidates' *habitus*. In this regard, Bourdieu's (1986) theory defines habitus, as the embodied state of cultural capital. As mentioned, it presupposes a process of incorporation that starts from early domestic education. Habitus is converted into an integral part of the person. Its acquisition is disguised and functions as symbolic capital, meaning that it tends to be unrecognised as a form of capital and it is seen as a legitimate competence. The habitus frames a way of thinking and acting, including body conduct, poise, bodily skills and competencies, the embodied aspects of language in speech habits, vocabulary, and accent (Wolkowitz, 2006: 20). All in all, it is what makes social agents behave in a specific way, according to the circumstances. Bourdieu's habitus is context based. The value given to embodied cultural capital changes according to the *field* and each field is marked by its own taken-for-granted understanding of the world, implicit and explicit rules of behaviour, and valuation of what confers power onto someone.

The previous chapter highlighted that habitus and especially middle/upper-class behaviour is especially valued in bodywork, including for being hired as a care assistant or a nurse. The examples of Shamrock and Dianella, highlight that habitus is also crucial in the selection of managers. To be selected candidates need to have the "gesture", "way of putting oneself", and the "tone of voice" that is valued in Shamrock's field. Conversely, to be hired by Dianella, the candidate will need to have the habitus valued in the recruiters' field and a common understanding of "courage".

Can migrant women's habitus and understandings fit in local recruiters' mental image of the position? Bourdieu (1986) puts emphasis on the fact that habitus can be transferred from one generation to another, and is "acquired" quite "unconsciously". However, Wolkowitz (2006: 176) stresses that nowadays people are more conscious of the grooming and surveillance of habitus. As a result, the "worked-up habitus of fields of labour" has become "more mindful". Workers can conform to work demands or distance themselves from them. Therefore, candidates should be able to work on their habitus and cultural capital to correspond to Shamrock's and Dianella's criteria.

When it comes to migrant candidates, who are outsiders to the fields of employment, a critical issue concerns their access to specific social and cultural capital. Perrotta (2014) highlights that migrants' habitus was formed in another context, namely in their country of birth. As a result, compared to candidates that were socialised in Shamrock's and Dianella's context, namely those born or who grew up in the same region, it might be more challenging for them to get to know what are the "postures and mannerisms" and "way of carrying oneself", that are valued in the selection process.

On the other hand, Perrotta (2014) also indicates that migrants' habitus might change through new socialisation that follows migration. Therefore, we could assume that migrant women might overcome the obstacles mentioned above, depending on their social network (whether they know persons familiar with the employment *fields*), and their cultural capital (whether they access information on how to behave). However, Perrotta (2014: 175) stresses that social actors cannot easily get rid of their own incorporated dispositions, which are "extremely resistant to change".

Moreover, we should add that modifying one's habitus can have implications in terms of symbolic violence. It might imply that the person recognises as legitimate the power that imposes specific ways of being and behaving. Conversely, it is also because migrants are familiar with other contexts, that they are more likely to be conscious about the symbolic violence that is at stake in the labour market, like in Shamrock's and Dianella's fields, while locals might remain blind to it.

4.3 Scrutinising Migrant Women's Bodies

My fieldwork put to light that the recruitment and selection process involves a high level of scrutiny over candidates' bodies, especially if they are migrant women. In this section, I highlight that the perception of bodies and the way they are racialised and *otherised* need to be contextualised. Participants in the study also stressed that *aesthetic* criteria have a significant impact on recruitment and selection, especially of female candidates and that they have contradictory implications when it comes to scrutinising migrant women's bodies.

Floating Racialisation and Otherness

Stuart Hall (2013) has stressed that *race*, which is a socially constructed category that does not exist in itself but has a social reality, in the sense that it produces effects on those persons who are racialised, is a floating signifier. The way in which racialising markers such as physiognomy, the colour of the skin but also culture and religion, amongst others, are interpreted changes depending on the context and on who looks at them.

Interviews with graduate women from Sub-Saharan Africa echo these reflections. For instance, Clemensia, who was born in Senegal and moved to France for her studies, felt that the way she was racialised changed depending on the context. From her perspective, blackness and whiteness were moving identities.

> *Our identities change, sometimes Black, sometimes white. In Africa, I can be French, white. Here [in France], I will be considered Black. Do I feel Black or not? It depends on the day. Sometimes I do Nappy [hair], in Afro mode. Sometimes I go: 'well, I want to have straight, curly hair'. Am I white sometimes, Black sometimes? I don't know. It's hybrid.* (Clemensia, born in Senegal, unemployed, France).

Callaia, who was born in Niger and also lived in France, referred to the fact that her interlocutors, especially at the workplace, continued to refer to her otherness as an African migrant woman even though she had lived in France for decades. Callaia introduced herself as *métissée* (mixed) but highlighted that her difference was "visible", compared to mine,[2] and estimated that this was the reason why she continued to be "classified in a category". Despite her professional position as a nurse and the time that had passed after first arriving in Alsace, patients at the hospital were regularly referring to her otherness.

> *I've been here since the 1990s, but I'm still seen as… It's when I'm with people… I don't realise. It's when I'm asked a question like: "By the way, how long have you been here? Are you used to food? Isn't it cold here?"; and I think: yeah, I'm not from here, but I'm not from there either, because I spent almost as much time there as here.* (Callaia, born in Niger, nurse, France).

When it comes to women from European non-Eu countries, the previous chapter stressed that although they might not be explicitly racialised as non-white, these women are also subject to forms of labelling. Participants' accounts highlighted that the process of othering is also floating and context-based. A relevant example that was mentioned was that of Viola, who was born in Russia. Viola indicated that she felt she *became* a migrant from Eastern Europe when arriving in Italy. The verb that Viola used emphasises the fact that her becoming *other* was a process that needs to be contextualised in time and space. Before moving to Italy, she was labelled neither as a migrant nor as being from Eastern Europe.

Moreover, Veronica, who was born in Ukraine and lived in Veneto, connected the fact of being otherised to the visual perception of racialisers. As such, her account stressed that the way European women from non-Eu countries could be perceived in Italy also corresponded to a form of racialisation, which shared some features with the racialisation of Black women in the Italian and French contexts.

> *Not every day, but almost, somewhere someone tells me I'm a* foreigner. *Because anyway I speak Italian but there is, anyway, the face is not Italian at all. So they also recognise me by [my] face.* (Veronica, born in Ukraine, business manager, Italy)

---

[2] Callaia indicated that, as a French and Colombian, I was mixed (*métisse*) like her, but that in my case my mixing was not visible (*ça se voit pas*).

'She Has to be Pretty'

Scholars have highlighted that beauty and attractiveness are embedded in power relations that involve racialisation, class, and gender. Women's beauty is steeped in class inequalities, as well as colonial and patriarchal discourses that privilege whiteness, heterosexuality, youth, and the upper class (Mears, 2014: 1334). When it comes to the impact of beauty in accessing employment, scholars' positions are divided. Green (2013: 152) estimates that sexual attractiveness benefits women only "minimally if at all in the employment sector". Mears (2014: 1339), instead, indicates that women can be both penalised for being unattractive as well as too attractive, but what remains steady is the "high level of scrutiny of their bodies".

My fieldwork confirms that beauty matters in the selection process. Both in Alsace and Veneto, recruiters referred to the prettiness of female candidates as a characteristic that was required or at least appreciated. Interviewees highlighted the importance of aesthetics in different variants of *bodywork*, including for positions as care assistants and nurses. Senecio, a recruiter in Veneto, described a specific selection process for a nurse position. Senecio stressed that his client, the director of a retirement home, tended to intervene to make sure he would select an attractive female candidate.

> *Even when we were in job selection contests, now and then, the director came in. […] When the nurse was pretty, young, [he was] saying '[a candidate] like that goes very well'. If maybe [the female candidate] was over 45 [years old], with a tone of voice a little bit… imperative, and maybe not particularly interesting from a physical point of view, [he would say] 'But is this one okay? Are we sure?'* (Senecio, recruiter, Italy).

Senecio also indicated that in several sectors, including for jobs that do not involve bodywork, if a woman is to be hired, she needs to be 'pretty':

> *I realise that in many contexts, in many situations but also very normal service companies rather than manufacturing, […] when they have to select a woman, mainly, she has to be pretty. […] Many selections are made not based on*

> *experiences, skills but are made based on what you tell me, on what impression you make on me, a little on the gut feeling.* (Senecio, recruiter, Italy).

Similarly, in Alsace, Elm described the selection of a candidate for a position as a scientist within his organisation. Elm mentioned that the candidate was "perfectly competent in the technical field" and that she was also "very pretty". Would have he made the same comment if it was a male candidate? Elm's example suggests that the aesthetic criterion goes beyond bodywork, as the woman was hired for a scientific position.

> *She was a very pretty young Black woman, too. [...] But hey, she was very strong, very strong. She wasn't recruited for [her] pretty face. She had very good results in writing, and she did an absolutely excellent interview. Perfectly bilingual. Perfectly competent in the technical field.* (Elm, recruiter, France).

The analysis has emphasised the impact of aesthetic criteria in the recruitment and selection process. We can wonder how recruiters in the Alsatian and Veneto contexts define prettiness, especially in terms of racialisation and class. When it comes to class, an interesting observation came from the experience of Sirelli, who worked as a recruiter in Veneto. Sirelli told me about a recruitment and selection process in which she was asked to select a group of hostesses. Mears (2014: 1333) classify this job as part of *aesthetic labour*, as appearance is a central component of the wage, and workers commodify their bodies. In her example, Sirelli explained that clients were looking for hostesses of "a superior level". Sirelli description encompasses aesthetic criteria, language skills and a habitus that could be associated with the middle/upper class.

> *The staff they were looking for were hostesses, but not hostesses as 'figurines', hostesses who had a specific type of standing, who spoke English very well, and who also had a confident attitude in the relationship. [...] I found some people, some people who were very much in line with that research, so the kind of wannabe models, yeah, who spoke perfect English, who had had international experiences, with higher education and so on.* (Sirelli, recruiter, Italy).

Interestingly, Sirelli's example stressed how gender and class habitus intersect and become a selection criterion in aesthetic labour. On the other hand, it highlights that recruiters associate higher education with bearing a middle/upper-class habitus. As a result, having tertiary education can be appreciated when accessing aesthetic labour, as education might function as a proxy to select workers with such a habitus. The following section focuses on how aesthetic criteria intersect with racialisation and is influenced by essentialism resulting from the colonial past.

Eroticisation of Migrant Women Bodies

Both in Alsace and Veneto, scholars have highlighted that colonialism went hand in hand with the whitening of national identities and that the construction of racial models was gendered (Ndiaye, 2008; Dorlin, 2014; Petrovich Njegosh & Scacchi, 2012). While white women tended to be depicted as "pure", colonised women tended to be eroticised. In Italy, Petrovich Njegosh and Scacchi (2012: 44) notes that Italian women were depicted as innocent victims, while colonised Black women were portrayed as "hyper-sexualised preys". In France, scholars have underlined how the colonial project went hand in hand with the appropriation and eroticisation of colonised bodies, in particular, that of women (Dorlin, 2014). In both contexts, scholars stress that the eroticisation of colonial subjects, particularly women, continues to mark the collective imaginary. Fieldwork highlights that this trend does not only concern women from former colonies. It also regards women from other "peripheral locations" (Grosfoguel et al., 2015) that were not directly colonised but that are also racialised and essentialised.

In Italy, women from both non-EU Europe and Sub-Saharan Africa indicated that they felt eroticised by locals. Migrant women with tertiary education believed they were perceived as *playgirls*, women of easy virtue or husband-stealers. In this regard, they referred to symbolic and verbal violence to which they were exposed. For instance, Veronica, who was born in Ukraine, and Rose, who was born in Congo, specifically mentioned the interactions they have had with unknown persons in the public sphere. Veronica referred to an episode at the beginning of her stay in Italy.

> *I remember it struck me. I went to pay at the post office, it was still at the beginning, and because of the accent, 'Where are you from?'. I said 'from Ukraine'. 'Ah, yeah because you Ukrainian women steal our Italian males'. I said: 'I have not stolen anything from anyone'.* (Veronica, born in Ukraine, business manager, Italy).

Similarly, Rose felt that Black African women tended to be associated with the sex work industry:

> *The difficulty I have faced as a foreign woman was when, for example, you also… because, for Westerners, the majority of women come to work in prostitution. […] For them, we are African women so maybe I am here to look for money. So maybe I'm a street woman. So, sometimes they approach you and all that, proposing [to do] stuff even in the middle of the day.* (Rose, born in Congo, unemployed, Italy).

The eroticisation of women born in non-EU Europe and Sub-Saharan Africa, as well as their exposure to symbolic and verbal violence, echoes the findings of Toffanin (2015). The scholar studies how Latin-American women are *hyper-sexualised* in the Italian context (Ibid: 101). Toffanin highlights that this process is embedded in gender, racial, and class relations. It connects to stereotypes regarding country of birth, physical appearance and "projections" of different "femininity models compared to the alleged Italian 'standard'" (Ibid: 99). According to these projections, Latin American women would be more accessible by nature, culture, or social and economic status, as migrant women are perceived as belonging to the working class. My fieldwork stresses that this phenomenon does not only concern Latin American women, but rather affects a broader group of women, including women from European non-EU countries and Sub-Saharan Africa.

In France, female recruiters and social workers also made an implicit reference to the trend of eroticising migrant women by referring to *exoticism*. Dianella, a recruiter in Alsace, mentioned the hiring of a Colombian graduate woman in her company. As mentioned, the recruiter indicated that her colleagues accepted the woman well, because Colombia sounded exotic.

And for specific origins [of female candidates], well, I think managers can invent pretexts and they might not always be open-minded. Colombia was fine because Colombia sounds a bit exotic. (Dianella, recruiter, France).

Similarly, Daphne, a social worker in Alsace, considered that women were preferred over men when accessing positions in the context of diversity management. In her view, this trend was due to the fact that migrant women were eroticised for looking exotic, especially if they were Black. Daphne's comment also highlights class expectation, as she associated exoticism with *elegance*, and *finesse*, attributes that tend to be associated with middle/upper-class habitus.

I caricature for you to understand. Ok, she is Black, but behind there is elegance, there is a finesse, it will give exoticism to the company. We will enter our quota for the number of foreigners tanned. If you are taking some, you might better take a woman. But because they, it's clearly sexist and purely... It's a shame, but it's the truth. (Daphne, social worker, France).

Daphne also stressed that, although migrant women might be hired in the context of diversity management, they might not access positions as managers. From her perspective, the hiring of *diverse* candidates is limited to low and intermediary jobs. Her comment echoes the reflection of Mears (2014) on aesthetic labour. As mentioned, this segment of the labour market encompasses jobs in which individuals are compensated, indirectly or directly for their own body's looks and affects. Aesthetic labour includes positions such as sales assistants in the retail industry. In this context, workers' bodies are controlled and commodified by the company. Meads notes that women are the "frontline aesthetic labours". However, their work does not translate into earning power, and their access to managerial positions remains limited. From her viewpoint (Mears, 2014: 1338), the value of women's bodies tends to accumulate to men, as they are the majority of owners in the service and sex industries. Mears' (2014) analysis can be transposed to our analysis: our fieldwork data put to light that, in the context of diversity management, the value of the bodies of racialised and eroticised migrant women is essentially monetized by managers, who are mainly men, white, and upper class.

While Dianella and Daphne highlighted the potential working advantages of looking "exotic", Black migrant women both in France and Italy emphasised that they felt they were requested to mitigate their blackness when looking for employment. For instance, Clemensia, who was born in Senegal and was looking for a job in Alsace, indicated that when going to job interviews she felt her hairstyle was being judged by recruiters, as *nappy* hair was not being considered positively. Clemensia felt that there was pressure for non-white people to look like whites. She described it as a call for *jacksonisation*: Like Michael Jackson, Blacks would be expected to change their bodies to look as white as possible.

> *Does the French society, to finally integrate young people, want everyone to jacksonise, [or] what? That everyone becomes Michael Jackson, that we get a nose job. My nose is flat, it is flat; it is fat, it is fat. It's not* baguette... *it cannot be, because my ancestors are Black and we, in our case, our phenotype it's like that. So, I will not uncurl, change the colour of my skin, get a nose job, remove my lips, remove my buttocks... I mean, become the same, finally... such as the West proposes it.* (Clemensia, born in Senegal, unemployed, Alsace).

In Italy, Rose, who was born in Congo, shared Clemensia's feelings. However, Rose believed that appearance and middle-/upper-class habitus mitigated racial stereotyping. Rose's comment touches upon the intrinsic relationship between racialisation and class which was highlighted in the 1950s in Frantz Fanon's (2008) *Black Skin, White Mask* and continues to be topical.

> *So, when I show up at a job interview, I always manage to maybe put on my little skirt, my little heels and everything, well, make-up and everything. So I pay attention to appearance when it comes to job interviews. [...] So, for me appearance counts because even if you are Black but you are well dressed, you express yourself well, the first impact you leave, well, it is the physical [aspect], the way you are dressed.* (Rose, born in Congo, unemployed, Italy).

* * *

Overall, this chapter has highlighted the multiple impacts that essentialism has in the recruitment and selection process. It stressed that skills are being valued according to who embodies them and the process is influenced by essentialism based on gender, racialisation, and class. More specifically, the chapter studied in detail the impact of essentialism on the assessment of education, experience, language skills, and soft skills. Through this accurate analysis, the chapter has emphasised that skills are not objective assets, but that they are socially constructed.

Moreover, the analysis has stressed that the physical body of female candidates is subject to high scrutiny, as they are often expected to be pretty. More specifically, the chapter has emphasised that both in France and Italy, migrant women's bodies are subject to a contradictory process of eroticisation and injunction of whitening. In the context of diversity management, it was stressed that the value of the bodies of racialised and eroticised migrant women is monetised by managers, who are mainly men, white, and upper class. At the same time, migrant women, and especially Black women, felt that they were compelled to mitigate their blackness when looking for employment.

References

Babić, V., & Slavković, M. (2011). Soft and hard skills development: A current situation in Serbian companies. In: *Proceedings of the Management, Knowledge and Learning International Conference.*

Bauder, H. (2003). "Brain abuse", or the devaluation of immigrant labour in Canada. *Antipode, 35*(4), 699–717.

Bourdieu, P. (1986). The forms of capital. *Cultural Theory: An Anthology, 1*(2011), 81–93.

Chiswick, B. R., & Miller, P. W. (2009). The international transferability of immigrants' human capital. *Economics of Education Review, 28*(2), 162–169.

Cuban, S. (2013). *Deskilling migrant women in the global care industry.* Palgrave Macmillan.

De Rudder, V., & Vourc'h, F. (2006). Les discriminations racistes dans le monde du travail. In D. Fassin & E. Fassin (Eds.), *De la question sociale à la question raciale? Représenter la société française.* La Découverte.

Dorlin, E. (2014). *La matrice de la race. Généalogie sexuelle et coloniale de la Nation française*. La Découverte.

Fanon, F. (2008). *Black skin, white masks*. Grove press.

Foucault, M. (1991). *Discipline and punish: The birth of the prison*. Penguin.

Garrouste, C. (2008). Language skills and economic returns. *Policy Futures in Education, 6*(2), 187–202.

Green, A. I. (2013). 'Erotic capital' and the power of desirability: Why 'honey money' is a bad collective strategy for remedying gender inequality. *Sexualities, 16*(1–2), 137–158.

Grosfoguel, R., Oso, L., & Christou, A. (2015). 'Racism', intersectionality and migration studies: Framing some theoretical reflections. *Identities, 22*(6), 635–652.

Hall, S. (2013). *Identités et cultures 2. Politiques des différences*. Editions Amsterdam.

Hochschild, A. R. (2012). *The managed heart: Commercialization of human feeling*. University of California Press.

Isphording, I. E. (2013). Returns to foreign language skills of immigrants in Spain. *Labour, 27*, 443–461.

Kofman, E. (2012). Gender and skilled migration in Europe. *Cuadernos de Relaciones Laborales, 30*(1), 63–89.

Lehtovaara, H., & Jyrkinen, M. (2021). Skilled migrant women's experiences of the job search process. *Nordic Journal of Working Life Studies, 11*, 11–30.

Lo, W. Y. W. (2011). Soft power, university rankings and knowledge production: Distinctions between hegemony and self-determination in higher education. *Comparative Education, 47*(2), 209–222. https://doi.org/10.1080/03050068.2011.554092

McDowell, L. (2011). *Working bodies: Interactive service employment and workplace identities* (Vol. 61). John Wiley & Sons.

Mears, A. (2014). Aesthetic labor for the sociologies of work, gender, and beauty. *Sociology Compass, 8*(12), 1330–1343.

Mezzadra, S., & Neilson, B. (2013). *Border as method, or, the multiplication of labor*. Duke University Press.

Ndiaye, P. (2008). *La condition noire. Essai sur une minorité française*. Calmann-Lévy.

Perrotta, D. (2014). Violenza simbolica e migranti in Italia. Esperienze di ricerca con operai rumeni e braccianti burkinabé. *Rassegna italiana di sociologia, 55*(1), 149–180.

Petrovich Njegosh, T., & Scacchi, A. (2012). *Parlare di razza. La lingua del colore tra Italia e Stati Uniti*. Ombre corte.

Scrinzi, F. (2013). *Genre, migrations et emplois domestiques en France et en Italie. Construction de la non-qualification et de l'altérité ethnique*. Pétra.

Toffanin, A. M. (2015). *Controcanto. Donne latinoamericane tra violenza e riconoscimento*. Guerini Scientifica.

Ufficio Statistica della Regione Veneto. (2018). Il Veneto si racconta, il Veneto si confronta. *Rapporto statistico anno 2018, Specialita'*. Available at: http://statistica.regione.veneto.it/Pubblicazioni/RapportoStatistico2018/pdf/sintesi.pdf

Wolkowitz, C. (2006). *Bodies at work*. Sage.

5

"I can't Limit my Life to your Prejudices". Coping and Resistance Strategies

Rosamel grew up in a medium city in Cameroon. When she finished secondary school, her parents decided that she would study abroad, as her brothers and sisters had done. The first option was France, but as there were no opportunities to apply for a study visa in that country, Rosamel's parents opted for Italy. After passing linguistic and career entrance tests, Rosamel started studying physiotherapy in Veneto. She graduated after three years of being in Italy and started looking for employment in her field. Rosamel remembers she was going from one cooperative to the other, leaving her resume.

> *It's not like I had an appointment. I carried my resume everywhere. "Yeah, put it there". I used to think: "'Put it there' is it because you don't care, just to be done with me, or are you working and busy?". Anyway, you still feel prejudice. And in that, you should never give up, no matter how, this is my conviction. The prejudice of the other, or the difficulty that the other has to see me as I am, for what I am, cannot prevent me from doing what I have to do. I can't limit my life to your prejudices. I can't take that load; it's not up to me. And so, I continued carrying it everywhere.* (Rosamel, born in Cameroon, physiotherapist, Italy).

A.-I. Romens, *Deconstructing Essentialism*,
https://doi.org/10.1007/978-3-031-14399-1_5

Thanks to her persistence, Rosamel managed to work continuously as a physiotherapist after graduating. Although she felt that interlocutors in cooperatives were eventually essentialising her, Rosamel refused to internalise the negative label. She had confidence in her working capacities and felt she could find work in her field. Like Rosamel, migrant women with tertiary education react in very different ways to the essentialist processes that affect them.

The literature has studied how people react to stigmatisation and essentialism. Departing from Goffman's (1990) and Allport's (1979) analysis of stigma and prejudice, part of the scholarship proposes to think about stigmatisation as a form of stress. According to the literature, this approach permits calling attention to how stigmatised people cope with the stress they endure as a consequence of their stigmatised status (Miller & Kaiser, 2001).

Scholars have highlighted that Goffman's (1990) approach and the analysis of coping strategies mentioned above tend to give little room to resistance. Accordingly, in Goffman's theory stigmatised individuals can hardly destigmatize themselves, or put forth their stigma as a "simple and not especially discredited difference" rather than a "failing" (Gussow & Tracy, 1968: 317). According to Goffman (1990 [1963]), individuals "manage" information about themselves, and "react", rather than resist or reject negative appraisals of others. Riessman (2000: 114) stresses that Goffman assumes that stigmatised persons hold the same belief about their condition as the rest of society, while there are countless instances in which individuals disavow dominant perspectives.

The chapter takes into account these critics and analyses the strategies enacted by migrant women to cope with essentialism and stratifications without questioning them, or conversely that resist and challenge these processes. The chapter analyses practices and strategies from an intersectional perspective, highlighting that they are interlocked. Migrant women do not follow a single path but might implement different practices and strategies at the same time. Moreover, these women might also change their views and expectations. As a result, practices and strategies might evolve along with their lives, based on their experiences. As suggested by Miller and Kaiser (2001: 88), women try several alternatives, and feedback from one response may alter other responses that are made. The first section of the chapter focuses on the way migrant women cope with essentialism and the second section studies how they cope with stratifications.

5.1 Coping, Resisting and Challenging Essentialism

The first section of the chapter focuses on how migrant women react to essentialism. These strategies might challenge the dominant ideology, but this is not always the case. Moreover, they are also interlocked, as migrant women with tertiary education do not follow a single path, but they might implement different strategies simultaneously and throughout their lives.

Differentiating and Distancing

Scholars have emphasised that stigmatised persons may turn to sympathetic others who share their stigma (Goffman, 1990). As a result, disadvantage can be used as a basis for creating community. However, stigma might also stimulate practices of internal social differentiation and distancing from the stigmatised group (Wacquant, 2008). For instance, migrants might *internalise* stereotypical representations of the dominant group and react to essentialism by differentiating and distancing themselves from co-nationals or sympathetic others who are perceived with disdain (Moroşanu & Fox, 2013: 440).

The strategy of distancing and stigmatising a group with which one is associated was also identified in my fieldwork. This coping strategy reproduced forms of essentialism which were transferred to other stigmatised groups of migrants. For instance, Rose, who was born in Congo and lived in Italy, felt that African women tended to be associated with sex work. In order to cope with essentialism, Rose transferred the stigma to Nigerian women. In doing so, she reproduced a negative, essentialist discourse, and dissociated from a group still defined in a gendered, national and racialised way.

> *Because, for Westerners, the majority of women come for prostitution. Because Nigerians… it's Nigerians who do that. I am Congolese. Well, as it is difficult for them to distinguish… nationalities, Congolese, Nigerians, Ivorians* (Rose, born in Congo, unemployed, Italy).

Echoing the literature (Moroşanu & Fox, 2013), the second strategy of distancing that was identified in my fieldwork corresponds to referring to personal success and contrasting it with the failure of other co-nationals. The strategy was used by Yasmin in Italy. However, in contrast with the findings of Moroşanu and Fox (2013), Yasmin did not only refer to her individual success and skills. She rather divided the group of Ukrainian graduate women between those who had "clear objectives" and the will to work in their field, and those who "relax[ed]" and failed in finding employment in line with their studies. Yasmin blamed graduate Ukrainian women who were deskilled for their position in the job market: if they only had access to jobs with low social recognition, it was because they were not sufficiently determined to access other jobs.

> *Because [those] who start from below already give up certain things. A girl I know who works in [city], she would be a professional I don't say a programmer, but she could have another job in a company, but she's stuck there, caring for people. She did not go further to make her degree recognised [in Italy]; in my opinion, it is unthinkable. She was at the polytechnic university, she was already teaching, but she did this reverse, probably to make her life easier. I mean that some try. I see in the Facebook group of Ukrainians in Italy, that those between 25 and 40 [years old], look a bit for redemption from this point of view. […] This is the generation that tries to make redemption of what they used to have. Some instead relax completely, understand that this is their [new] reality, and leave it that way. […] If a person has clear objectives, she succeeds in getting what she wants.* (Yasmin, born in Ukraine, business manager, Italy).

The third strategy of distancing consisted of differentiating by arguing closeness to the dominant majority. An example was provided by Amaryllis, who was born in Armenia and lived in France. The woman had internalised a negative discourse on migrants, according to which they represented a threat to the (local white) population. Although Amaryllis partly identified with the migrant group, she also distanced herself from it, by putting forward arguments based on her administrative status, ties, and living experience in France. Amaryllis' account had several implications concerning the internalisation of a negative and essentialist discourse towards migrants. Firstly, she perceived migration as an "uncontrolled" problem, although she did not explicitly indicate why the phenomenon would alarm locals. Secondly, she excluded migrants from her representation of the local population and defined the legitimate locals according to their bloodline.

> *I can really give evidence of this enormous, this phenomenon, it is hard again, this phenomenon of migration. […] I always found that it's uncontrolled. […] Frankly, the population suffers. The people who have lived here for centuries, we will say that. Nobody talks about it. And I allow myself to talk about it because precisely I am not from here. Well, I hold the [French] citizenship. So I can take a bit of the defence of the population… who says that "this country belongs to me", "used to belong to me". […] Of course, I feel French, because since I have my children, who are French, since I have French citizenship, after 16 years and… […] It is my vocation to give evidence. To tell how it's going, and why not also say things more honestly than people… how to say, who welcome. The people who welcome [migrants] are the French who have always lived here* (Amaryllis, born in Armenia, tutor, France).

When it comes to distancing, Amaryllis presented herself as being in the middle between migrants and locals. Although she stressed that she would always have an "immigrant touch", she distinguished herself by pushing forward her *Frenchness*, connected to the fact that she had acquired French citizenship, her partner and children were French, and she had lived for 16 years in the country. From her perspective, the fact of being in-between gave her the legitimacy to give a negative - and essentialist - description of migrants.

Resistance Thinking

In contrast with the previous coping strategy, migrant women might also resist labelling and stereotyping. However, their resistance practices might not be visible, as they might not always perceive that openly challenging essentialism is a possibility (Riessman, 2000). Speaking out and taking action might represent a risk that varies depending on their subjectivity but also on their labour status, and their economic, social, cultural and symbolic capital. When migrant women feel that they have too much to lose if they openly challenge essentialism, they might still oppose the dominant wisdom by implementing resistance thinking.

An example that illustrates the tension between resistance thinking and the impossibility to act openly was given by Rosanna, who was born in Cameroon and studied economics in Italy. When I met her, Rosanna was working as a care assistant in Veneto and felt that African women tended to be relegated to the bottom of the employment structure. Although Rosanna was sceptical about the possibility of accessing jobs in her field in Italy, she blamed recruiters and did not question her capacities. However, in her daily interactions at work, she felt that she could not openly reply to verbal provocations.

> *Now I work as a care assistant, but I don't want to end my days there. No. Because if I'm honest, I did it because I couldn't find a job in my field. Although I like this job so much, let's say, it's very physically demanding. Also psychologically, because there is a different approach when you are a foreigner. So you need to have a lot, a lot, a lot of patience because you get so many bad and bad words. However, it is the workplace; you always have to smile. And not just from patients, [but] even from colleagues. So it's not a place where I want to finish.* (Rosanna, born in Cameroon, care assistant, Italy).

Rosanna's work ethic, but also her precarious labour status, the fact that she needed an income, and her power position in the *field* discouraged her from acting openly. From her perspective, acting out involved a significant loss, a risk she did not want to take. Moreover, her account also emphasises the emotional labour (Hochschild, 2012) that migrant women perform when facing essentialism, as she had to continue smiling despite the verbal violence to which she was exposed.

In addition to resistance thinking, migrant women were also eventually implementing a complementary strategy consisting of putting the fault on the blamers. To discredit those who essentialise, and affirm migrant women's worth, interviewees tended to emphasise the lack of cultural capital of blamers. For instance, Winika, who was born in Ukraine and worked as a pizza maker in Italy, disregarded her colleagues for their low level of education.

> *There was at work, but out of the precise context of work, because of this ignorance I was telling you, ignorance connected to [their] poor education, there are people that [are] really nationalists, racists.* (Winika, born in Ukraine, pizzaiola, Italy).

Although women had experienced downward social mobility, they reaffirmed their class superiority compared to blamers by referring to their higher level of education, or their class position before migration. In this regard, Vianello (2014: 92) indicates that in Soviet countries, in which Soviet citizens were considered equal owners of the means of production, education was "one of the main factors of social stratification".

Migrant women also stressed their superiority compared to blamers by highlighting their knowledge of different contexts. They stressed that they had had the opportunity to travel, and increase their knowledge about different contexts, while the blamers had never seen anything new. By doing so, migrant women were highlighting their superiority in terms of cultural capital and mobility power (Alberti, 2014). In my fieldwork, this strategy was adopted by Callaia in Alsace and Winika in Veneto.

> *If people have this imagination, it is not even by malice. It's just because they have… I say to myself, "I'm lucky, I left my country, I came". So I got to know something else, […] they did not share anything, they stayed amongst them.* (Callaia, born in Niger, nurse, France).
>
> *Until the end of life, I think they will be like this. They don't travel, they don't encounter anything new, because people open up when they see differences. I say as soon as you come out of a trip, you have already seen the world, a different world.* (Winika, born in Ukraine, pizzaiola, Italy).

Denigrating the blamers also involved forms of essentialism that tackled the dominant majority. To assert their superiority in response to essentialism, graduate migrant women also referred to the lack of merits of locals. For instance, they found that locals had opportunities within easy reach, while migrants had to fight to access resources and employment. By doing so, migrant women stressed their independence compared to the infantilised locals. The strategy was particularly visible in the context of the Italian *familist* welfare model (Lyon, 2006). For instance, Raisa, who was born in Cameroon and occasionally worked as a cultural mediator in Veneto, adopted this coping strategy. At the end of the interview, when the recorder was off, Raisa gave details on her views on Italians. From her perspective, Italians could afford to refuse a job because they lived "at their grandmother's", and could use their "grandfather's car". She contrasted this situation with that of migrants, who could not afford to refuse any employment, as they had to pay for everything, and were not otherwise financially supported.

Strategic Avoidance

To protect themselves from the violence of essentialism, migrant women may choose to avoid specific persons or spaces. This response to essentialism enables migrant women to avoid unpleasant confrontations, but at the same time, it also risks contributing to the reproduction of inequalities. Indeed, avoidance strategies run the danger of "self-imposed exile" (Riessman, 2000). On the other hand, it also enables migrant women to look for *safe spaces*, where they can resist objectification (Collins, 2000).

In my fieldwork interviews, migrant women indicated that they were avoiding sending their resumes for positions for which they found they had little chance of being hired. This practice corresponds to what De Rudder and Vourc'h (2006: 181) call *anticipatory rationalisation* which prevents candidates from presenting their application for specific positions to avoid a "humiliating confrontation". In my fieldwork, anticipatory rationalisation was often the result of previous negative experiences. Two examples were that of Cassia, who had studied management and ICT in Senegal and lived in France; and that of Rosanna, who was born in Cameroon and studied economics in Italy. They both tried to find employment in their fields, but their attempts failed. As a result, Cassia had stopped looking for employment when I met her, while Rosanna was focusing on intermediary positions in the care sector.

I was disappointed anyway; I had even stopped applying. Until... until now I'm not looking anymore. I wait to see what I can do and how to do it so that it can be productive, because it's useless to undertake, um, studies, which in the long run are useless. And that in the end, you do not like what you do. That's it. So, I was really disillusioned. Because I didn't think it was going to be as hard as it is, that it was going to be... as discriminating as it is. (Cassia, born in Senegal, unemployed, France).

Well, in [my] field of studies, indeed, I never found anything. Never. And then I got tired; I said 'what's the point'. And therefore, I no longer searched in my field. I was just looking for... I was just looking [for work] as a care assistant. (Rosanna, born in Cameroon, care assistant, Italy).

Both Cassia and Rosanna's accounts correspond to strategic avoidance, but their strategy also served different purposes. In the case of Cassia, the fact of stopping her job hunting enabled her to save energy to reflect on strategies that would facilitate access to the positions she wanted. Conversely, Rosanna's avoidance aimed at focusing her employment searches on positions that seemed easier to access. By targeting specific jobs, migrant women avoid unpleasant confrontations and wasting time, but they also contribute to the reproduction of the labour market stratifications.

Migrant Women's Mobility Power

Migrant women might also take action to resist and challenge essentialism, by leaving a setting in which they feel essentialised. This reaction is different from strategic avoidance: although it also aims at avoiding unpleasant confrontations, leaving a place implies that action is being taken. The absence of the person transforms the setting and interactions within a *field*. Scholars have stressed that migrants' *mobility power*, namely their capacity to move within the labour market and transnationally, permits them to resist precarious working conditions (Alberti, 2014). I argue that it is also an act of resistance that challenges essentialism and dominant wisdom. Moreover, it also permits migrant women to resist the stratifications of the labour market by refusing assignments at the bottom of the employment structure.

Quitting a Job One striking strategy consists of quitting a job, which might involve a significant financial loss, as the person stops receiving her salary. However, the economic impact of following such a path varies significantly depending on migrant women's economic capital (such as savings), social capital (who can financially and emotionally support them), and the possibilities they foresee to find another job or an alternative source of income.

In my fieldwork, Callaia, who was born in Niger and worked as a nurse in France, indicated that she quit her previous position at the hospital because of her manager's attitude. It should be stressed that Callaia did not resign, but asked to be transferred to another service within her organisation. Thanks to her job security, she felt empowered so to leave a setting in which she was feeling essentialised.

> *I saw that it was never fine until I asked to have an interview with [the manager]. [...] I said "There is something I do not understand", I said: "You always have something to blame me for, there is always this and that". [...] Then finally, she said to me that actually... I release a calm that disturbs her. I am unfazed, I smile and... So when she told me that [...], I thought "But, I cannot change, I'm like that, if that's how she perceives me and that's what disturbed her, I cannot change". "Well", I said, "Well, in this case, I'm leaving". And I asked to leave.* (Callaia, born in Niger, nurse, France).

In my fieldwork, migrant women were also leaving their jobs to resist the stratifications and refuse assignments in posts that were not in line with their educational background. Similarly to strategic avoidance, this strategy also permitted them to conserve energy and take time to think about the paths that could enable them to access more satisfying work. An example was provided by Rose, who studied communication sciences in Italy and started working in the cleaning sector to support her family. After several years of working in that sector, Rose quit her job as she was feeling frustrated and felt it did not value her studies.

> *I already had a family, so I had to quit [an internship] and do the cleaning. I was doing it for almost ten years. Almost ten years, yeah. Until I said: "No, it's enough ". I have studied. I cannot continue doing this kind of work... not only because my body was not holding up to it anymore, I had back pains, pains in*

my knees, pains a bit everywhere, let's say... I had to stop recently... This year, I resigned. (Rose, born in Congo, unemployed, Italy).

Onward Migration Besides quitting one's job, another way of leaving a set of circumstances consists of moving to another city or country. This response to essentialism is a way migrant women have to 'vote with their feet', meaning that it might reveal their "preferences about the desirability of alternative locations" (Faggian et al., 2011). Participants in my fieldwork mentioned their wish to move to other countries or other cities within the country, where they perceived they would be less essentialised and would have more chances to access graduate positions.

In my fieldwork, the wish to move to a more 'open context' was mentioned both in France and Italy, particularly by women who felt racialised as Blacks. For instance, Rada, who was born in Cameroon and worked in Veneto as a social support assistant, was eventually considering moving to countries such as France and Belgium where she estimated that her skills could be more valued.

> *And making the comparison precisely with [France and Belgium], I said to myself "but there are countries where you can easily integrate the world of work", in relation to your merit, in relation to what you are capable of doing, you can find something. [...] So why not give it a try?* (Rada, born in Cameroon, social worker, Italy).

Similarly, in Alsace, migrant women who felt especially essentialised in local labour markets were considering moving to other countries or eventually to Paris, which was perceived as a more open global city. Clemensia, who was born in Senegal and was looking for employment in Alsace, shared this perception.

> *If France does not want me, well, I'll go to Canada, the United States, China... I do not know, I'll go anywhere in the world. Well, I think Paris, they are a little more cosmopolitan, so, I set my hopes on it* (Clemensia, born in Senegal, unemployed, France).

When working with Muslim migrant women in the Netherlands, Eijberts and Roggeband (2016) also observed that migrant women intended to leave the country as a response to stigmatisation. However, the scholars (Ibid: 142) found that the option of moving was less attractive to the women who had children, as they did not want to "uproot their children". Conversely, in my fieldwork, children were not always refraining women from moving. On the opposite, being mothers could further motivate them to move abroad as they did not want their children to endure the discrimination they had faced.

Migrant women, and especially those who felt racialised as Black, feared their children would live the same experience. As a consequence, they wanted to move to other localities perceived as being more open-minded, where they believed their children would have more opportunities. In my fieldwork, both Rada in Italy and Clemensia in France expressed their worries that their children could be discriminated against because of their skin colour. Rada already had two children and was wondering where to go next. Clemensia did not have children yet but also felt concerned about the issue.

> *My thoughts are not limited only to myself, but how can I put my children at ease, how can I put my family at ease. So I'm wondering. By making them grow up in this country, will they have the opportunity… not to live 'what I have lived', in quotes? Will it be different if we go elsewhere?* (Rada, born in Cameroon, social worker, Italy).
>
> *If I have children, the first thing I will do is, when they finish primary school, I will try to take them elsewhere. Because for me, the high school system, especially* lycée *[…] creates a machine to orientate. When you have a bit of an origin, a bit coloured, they tend a bit to orientate you towards coloured kinds of stuff, yeah, [such as] technical high schools, and so on, although statistically, it offers fewer opportunities.* (Clemensia, born in Senegal, unemployed, France)

Confronting Verbally

I mentioned that migrant women might not always feel that they can respond to verbal provocation. However, it also happens that they feel empowered to talk back. Their confidence depends on their working status, their economic, cultural, social and symbolic capital, and on the *field* where aggression happens. By confronting blamers verbally, migrant women challenge accusers and deconstruct stigma. An example was provided by Callaia, who was born in Niger and worked as a nurse in Alsace.

> *I often talk to my children when they come home, and they are unhappy because something happened. I try to tone them down by saying: "Don't let people walk all over you". That's what I've learned. In my first job, the second... until I changed, I came, I said to myself: "It's over!". [...] In the past, I would let it go... now I've learned that it does not work that way* (Callaia, born in Niger, nurse, France).

In her account, Callaia emphasised how her response to essentialism had changed over time. Compared to the past, when she used to "let it go", she now felt empowered to take a stand and speak out. In this regard, Riessman (2000) has observed that childless women in South India gain the confidence to react to stigma, through age, maturity, and education. Compared to when she arrived in Alsace, Callaia had not only acquired maturity and age, but she had also passed a competitive nursing exam which re-asserted her capacities. She had also accessed a graduate position, as a nurse in a public hospital, and gained economic stability. All these factors contributed to empowering her so to openly challenge essentialism.

Proving One's Worth

Another strategy to cope with essentialism consists of fostering human capital skills to prove one's worth (Miller & Kaiser, 2001). The practice includes the fact of perfecting language skills, even when migrant women are already fluent (Eijberts & Roggeband, 2016: 143). Learning the local language accurately has a double implication: on the one hand, it means that migrant women accept the call to "perfectly speak" the local language; on the other hand, it also challenges essentialism as migrant women might be able to give evidence that their language skills can be better than that of locals.

A relevant experience in this regard is that of Acacia, who was born in Moldova and worked as a leader at a community centre in Alsace. Her experience highlights how preconceptions might evolve and how migrant women cope with them. In her work, it happened that users and colleagues had doubts about her language skills in French. However, Acacia managed to change their minds, proving that she could be more accurate than them in grammar and spelling. This experience was a little victory for her.

> *They believe that if you have an accent, you don't have the necessary skills and abilities, or you are not up to [the work] [...]. Once I told [my colleagues], they were puzzled [by some language issue], and I explained how to write the verbs. [...] A foreign woman who tells you how to write, they did not believe me, I said: 'Check it [up]!'. And they checked and, after that, each time, they are always asking me.* (Acacia, born in Moldova, leader at a community centre, France).

Compensating responses also include returning to study in one's field in the country of migration to prove one's worth. The strategy also has a double implication: on the one hand, it means that migrant women accept that their foreign degree is undervalued at the local level; on the other hand, the strategy enables migrant women to regain confidence in their capacities, stopping the tongue-wagging of blamers.

Callaia enacted this strategy to react to the contempt of her supervisor who considered she was not capable of exercising her job properly. Callaia had attended a midwife school in Niger but was informed, after a long process, that her Nigerien degree would not enable her to work as a midwife in France, but as a nursing assistant in maternity. She started working at a hospital, where she felt harassed by her manager, who was continually doubtful of her capacities.

> *Whenever there was something, [my supervisor] humiliated me by showing that I was not good at what I was doing. Until I started to doubt... to doubt about myself. And, uh... it was terrible because I really felt harassed. I went to work reluctantly and all. And one day she passed like this and then she swayed me like that, and said: "There is the competitive nursing exam that... to do it". I said, "No, I do not want to be a nurse". Then finally, I took, I looked, and I said: "Well... ". I think she wanted to tell me that I'm not able to be a midwife here [in France]. [...] It was a challenge. I took it like that. Well, I registered, I did the competition, and I succeeded* (Callaia, born in Niger, nurse, France).

Succeeding at the competitive exam permitted Callaia to obtain cultural capital that was institutionally recognized in France (Bourdieu, 1986: 21) and regain confidence in her skills. It was a little victory for her that enabled her to silence blamers who would doubt her capacities.

Acting Collectively

To cope with essentialism, migrant women might also ally themselves with those who share their stigma in order to resist and challenge essentialism. Based on the analysis of the fieldwork, I identified that aggregating with co-nationals or other persons that share an experience of stigma might involve three different resistance and challenge practices.

The first strategy consisted of creating *safe spaces* (Collins, 2000), where migrant women could find supportive relationships that passed everyday knowledge on how to navigate essentialism and stratifications. For instance, Cliantha, who was born in Senegal and worked as a chambermaid in France, indicated that she had found support in the community of Senegalese students that lived in her city. This backing consisted of emotional support when she felt homesick, but also in sharing strategies to help her access employment in the region. It is thanks to her network that Cliantha found employment in the hospitality industry.

Similarly, Rosanna, who lived in Veneto, indicated that she was a member of an association that gathers Cameroonians from a specific region of the country. Like Cliantha, Rosanna highlighted that the group provided emotional support and shared information on how to navigate the Italian environment. Moreover, Rosanna indicated that solidarity among members included financial and academic support, as an acquaintance from the association helped her to study for her exams in mathematics.

> *We make small donations, if we can say that, something like that. If one has any difficulty, some... so let's say that when someone has something to rejoice about, we do it together, and when one has something to cry about, we do it together. Yes, since we are far from our beloved ones, then we consider this group a bit like our family, which we do not have here. [...] They helped me so much*

with advice because they had been in Italy for a long time. Also, with studying, because at a certain point, I had to approach one of my fellow citizens so that he supported me with mathematics because he was good at maths. (Rosanna, born in Cameroon, care assistant, Italy).

In my fieldwork, the second type of collective gathering consisted of self-organising to support migrant women's access to rights. An example was provided by Yasmin, who was born in Ukraine and had experience as a cultural mediator in Italy. Yasmin had volunteered in an association that aims at supporting Ukrainians in their access to rights and services. She was using the knowledge she had accumulated working as a cultural mediator to support co-national women.

A bit from personal experience because I came to Italy, I had to inform myself, and then as a cultural mediator, we had refresher courses and all the bureaucratic basis. Then I collaborated with a migrant association called [name]. We organised an information desk, and there I gave information to migrant women regarding documents, regarding the residence permit, many asked me how to bring their children here because they wanted to enrol them in university (Yasmin, business manager, Italy).

The third type of collective gathering identified in my fieldwork aimed at challenging negative stereotypes by promoting a positive image of stigmatised groups. An example was provided by Rosella who had participated in creating an NGO to promote the "beautiful side of Africa" and contrast the essentialist representations of African migrants that emerged in the 1990s.

We named the association [Flower] precisely... to show the beautiful side of Africa, to make Africa known, that Africa is not just criminality, it is not just... because here [in Italy], at a certain point, African means you're in prostitution, no. African means you are 'clandestino', therefore in crime. So with this association in our own small way we have tried to do the little we can... [...] We have made Africa known for its art, Africa as well as... Africa is food, Africa is also literature, Africa... In short, a little of African culture, trying to make people know about it (Rosella, born in the Democratic Republic of Congo, physician, Italy).

Practices such as that mentioned by Rosella aim at collectively deconstructing negative stereotypes, by promoting a positive image of a stigmatised group. These initiatives have a double implication: on the one hand, they do not prevent the emergence of stereotypes that reify a difference between locals and migrants; on the other hand, self-organising to promote counter-narratives of a stigmatised group is a way to challenge the dominant wisdom and empower the oppressed group. It makes it possible to conquer a stand in the political arena, push claims forwards and counterbalance power relationships.

Overall, the section highlighted how women coped, resisted, and eventually challenged essentialism and dominant wisdom. It was stressed that although all of the interviewees were not activists of movements that looked for changing the status quo, their everyday resistance practices also contributed to transforming society and to decolonising imaginaries (Vergès, 2019).

5.2 Coping with Labour Market Stratifications

After analysing how migrant women cope, resist and challenge essentialism, this section focuses on employment strategies and studies how these women cope with the stratifications of the labour market. The section aims at completing the paths identified by Liversage (2009) when studying the trajectories of *highly skilled* migrant women in Denmark. The following section analyses the ambivalent strategies enacted by migrant women to access employment, highlighting that they can both challenge or reproduce employment stratifications.

Accepting Stratifications

Taking 'Whatever Job' Depending on their economic and social capital, migrant women can feel that they *need* to work to support themselves and their families. Indeed, if they cannot count on economic or social capital (including partners, family, friends or acquaintances that can support them financially), migrant women might accept any job offer, including posts that do not value their education and experience. In my fieldwork, participants who enacted this strategy looked for any job that could provide income.

Moreover, it appeared that increase in family responsibilities, and more especially, the birth of a child often represented additional costs that pushed migrant women to take jobs with low social recognition. An example was provided by Rosella, who was born in the Democratic Republic of Congo and lived in Italy. She indicated that she had to postpone her studies in medicine to get a job when her child was born. Rosella worked for several years as a domestic worker before being able to return to her abandoned studies.

> *He was born, so I lost the [academic] year, he was born, and I understood… Because you understand what it means to be a mother when you have your own child, and the expense no, because a child, you understand what it means in terms of cost only when you have your own son. I understood… No, I had to work, because he was born with a milk allergy, not even my milk… And so I had to… he grew up only with soy milk that costs a fortune — a disaster, not even my milk he digested. Then, immediately to work.* (Rosella, born in the Democratic Republic of Congo, physician, Italy).

Different strategies were enacted to cope with the frustration of working in unsatisfactory positions some of which overlapped with those mentioned in the previous section, such as resistance thinking which permitted migrant women to reassert their worth although their job did not correspond to their educational background. Two additional strategies that aimed at coping with downgrading or permitting to make it more bearable are studied below.

Temporary Downgrading Scholars have stressed that temporality might mitigate the frustration connected to the fact of performing unsatisfactory employment. For instance, Vianello (2014) observes that migrant women might perceive their migratory experience as an "interlude" in their life, that aims to fulfil a specific objective such as that of accumulating economic capital. As a result, downward mobility is made more acceptable because it is perceived as being temporary and takes place in a foreign country. As a result, Vianello estimates that migrant women might feel that the downgrading does not radically impact their social status, as when returning to their country of birth, they might regain their previous social position.

My fieldwork also highlights that migrant women can perceive their migration as being temporary and feel that they can regain status through return migration. By stressing the possibility of regaining a rewarding social position in their country of birth, migrant women were referring to their mobility power (Alberti, 2014). The women who implemented this strategy tended to highlight that they had not migrated for necessity but rather because they wished to have experience in a new context. For instance, this is what explained Azalea, who used to work in business management in Russia and felt frustrated with her career in France.

> *Well, I thought I could always come back home. If it won't work, if I don't receive anything, I can always go [back] to Moscow [...], and something will be there for me. Just, you know, I tried to push my luck and see how it goes.* (Azalea, born in Russia, administrative assistant, France).

Women also adopted this coping strategy when they migrated in the context of family reunification. In this case, they highlighted that they did not exclusively move to join a partner, but that they also wanted to face new challenges in their careers. The possibility of moving back to their country of birth was perceived as an option that made temporary downgrading more acceptable. For instance, Cassia, who was working in Senegal as an administrative assistant and was unemployed in France, explained that she had moved to Alsace to join her partner. For Cassia, the possibility of moving back to Dakar was an option that made temporary downgrading more acceptable, although she was not fully sure she would access her previous status in Senegal.

> *Because in the end, I'm going back home. However, if I leave [France], I do not know if my post in Dakar will still be waiting for me. I do not know when I will return [to Dakar]. And when I leave, I would like to have a French diploma, and then professional experience, so that it will not be that difficult for me to find a job there.* (Cassia, born in Senegal, unemployed, France).

Intergenerational Upward Mobility It emerged from my fieldwork that migrant women also cope with downgrading by associating their temporary 'sacrifice' with the possibility of ensuring a satisfactory social position for their children. Indeed, it happened that migrant women accepted jobs that were not in line with their background in order to accumulate the economic capital necessary to sustain their children in having a career and a better social position, compared to that of their mothers. In this regard, Kofman and Raghuram (2015) have stressed that mothers are perceived as being responsible for the intergenerational transfer of class privileges. Following this reasoning, I argue that by investing in their children's education and career, migrant women are implementing a strategy that aims at ensuring intergenerational upward social mobility. This objective makes temporary downgrading more acceptable.

An example was provided by the experience of Winika, who used to teach music in Ukraine and was working in Italy as a pizza maker. Winika accepted her social and professional downgrading as a cost to pay so that her son would have a better social position in Italy compared to hers. When I met her, Winika's son had finished his studies and was living in Switzerland, she felt that she could focus once again on her career. She was enrolled in tertiary education in Italy and was eventually planning to move abroad. From her perspective, her temporary downgrading had enabled her son to have a rewarding career and experience upward social mobility.

> *I firmly had that plan of making him study here [in Western Europe]. You know, having a European situation and then… maybe I'm obstinate. So I sacrificed my husband to say so, we passed… but maybe even that, he went into a crisis [because] the activity did not correspond to his soul. So my son and I stayed here. He has now moved to Basel. Now I can also move somewhere else.* (Winika, born in Ukraine, pizza maker, Italy).

Interestingly, Winika contrasted her capacity to cope with downgrading and give priority to her child's upward mobility to the incapacity of her husband to do so. Her ability to work at any level to support her family was a source of pride that she contrasted with her partner's incapacity to do the same. Winika's capacity to cope with downgrading was connected to her sense of responsibility towards her family, and more specifically her child. In this case, gender ideology facilitated Winika's acceptance of working in an unsatisfactory job.

For instance, Winika put her capacity to cope with downgrading in gender terms: she compared her determinism in providing upward mobility to her son, and her acceptance of downgrading, to the fragility of her husband, who did not cope with it. While her partner decided to migrate back to Ukraine, she decided to stay in Italy and 'sacrifice' her marriage, stressing the substantial emotional implications of giving priority to her child's upward mobility.

> *I was living with my husband, then afterwards, he became ill, he had a psychiatric illness. Anyway, it is not easy. In my opinion, it is also connected to the change... because from a teacher, from a role you have in a society there, you pass... he was working irregularly on naval sites, you know, that every time you risk your life, all off the books work, endless working days. He had a mental imbalance, I had to bring him home, and we got divorced, because my son was already here. He said: "Let's go back there". I said: "No, you go back. If you find work, after that, we can talk about it". And I say: "My son is not a balloon, he just started to get inserted here", just when he started learning the language... from one country to another country, to a third country. What comes out then?* (Winika, born in Ukraine, studied music pedagogy in Ukraine, pizza maker, Italy)

Circumventing Recruiters' Essentialism

It emerged from my fieldwork that migrant women enacted different strategies that aimed at circumventing the recruiters' essentialist perceptions. Two strategies that go in this direction were identified, both of which had ambivalent outcomes as they could still reproduce stratifications.

Relying on Ambivalent Social Networks Scholars have highlighted the centrality of networks in defining work placement (Portes & Bach, 1985). However, in labour markets that are highly stratified based on gender, racialisation, migratory status and citizenship, relying on national networks can limit migrant women's access to jobs and confine them to positions at the bottom of the employment structure, namely in the care sector (Tognetti Bordogna, 2012).

My fieldwork highlighted that co-national networks can also facilitate access to intermediary positions. Depending on the labour market stratifications, relying on social capital also enables women to access graduate employment and eventually to circumvent essentialism in the recruitment and selection process. This was the experience of Amapola, who struggled to find employment in France, as employers were refusing to hire her because of her short-term residence permit for family reasons. Amapola finally succeeded in accessing a position in an international organisation, thanks to an acquaintance. Amapola's example illustrates that relying on social capital might enable migrant women to access positions that they found more satisfying. However, it also reproduces stratifications as migrant women might find jobs in sectors in which other co-nationals are already over-represented.

> *And then, I do not remember who told me that they were looking for someone [in the international organisation]. And I'm the only one… well, the only one… if I could have a chance, it was in an international organisation, where they were not going to look at my papers for… to give me a job. […] It was like word of mouth. So someone here… told a friend of mine that… "we are looking for someone for this project" and she put me in touch… I gave a CV, I had an interview, and it's like that.* (Amapola, born in Albania, administrative assistant, France).

In contrast with the social network of co-nationals, scholars tend to consider 'bridging ties' with natives as leading to 'better' jobs and occupational status (Lancee, 2012). In this sense, research has highlighted that a network of students met in local universities might permit migrant women to access positions more in line with their educational background (Killian & Manohar, 2015). For instance, in my fieldwork Rosamel, who was born in Cameroon and worked as a physiotherapist in Veneto, stressed that she found employment in her field, thanks to her peers. Together with former students, Rosamel was part of a group in which they eventually posted information on available jobs. Getting the information through this network enabled Rosamel to avoid unpleasant confrontations with intermediary agencies.

> *I had heard about [this job] I think through a female or male colleague who worked there, and I think through a message.[…]. Now we have a Whatsapp*

group, but back then it was messages. So I had heard about this thing through this word of mouth among us colleagues (Rosamel, Cameroon, physiotherapist, Italy).

Conversely, my fieldwork also stressed the limits of *strong* ties with natives when accessing employment (Moroşanu, 2016). For instance, women can have a native-born partner and be frequently in contact with their local family-in-law but the potential advantages of that network can be jeopardised by the violence that aims at isolating them. The literature on family and gender violence has brought to light that women and men have been socialised to accept the family structure in which they live, even when there is power unbalance, and relationships are based on domination and dependence (Toffanin, 2015). Power unbalance might be reinforced in the context of bi-national couples, when migrant women join local partners. The former might move by herself with no network, and limited knowledge about the context where she is about to live, whereas her partner can count on a more extent cultural and social capital at the local level.

An example of the ambivalence of *strong* ties was given by Viola, who used to have a rewarding social position in Russia and was living in Italy. Viola had moved to Veneto to unite with her Italian partner and lived in the same house as her mother-in-law. Before leaving Russia, Viola obtained a diploma to teach Russian as a foreign language. After moving to Veneto, the woman struggled to get information on how to become a language teacher in Italy. Viola was shocked when she understood that her sister-in-law worked in a school and that no one in the family-in-law had given her any information on the issue. In contrast with the silence of her family-in-law, it is an acquaintance with whom she had *weak* ties that informed her of the procedure to follow to become a teacher. Viola's experience stresses that in the context of family violence, *weak* ties can be more supportive than *strong* ones.

My mother-in-law told me: "You have to go to every school and bring your resume". I carried the curriculum but felt that there was something wrong. […] Only a year later, the girlfriend of a friend of my husband explained all these things to me, even though she does a different job. […] Later I realised that my mother-in-law knew it all and didn't even give me any suggestions, because the wife of my husband's brother works in a school. And nobody… I was very angry, really. (Viola, born in Russia, unemployed, Italy).

Taking Competitive Exams A second strategy that aims at circumventing recruiters' essentialist views consists of taking and eventually passing competitive exams. Migrant women perceived these recruitment procedures as being more neutral in terms of essentialism, compared to having a single recruiter assessing their curriculum vitae and conducting a job interview. However, my fieldwork highlighted that different obstacles can prevent migrant women from accessing competitive exams. For instance, having local citizenship and local diplomas can be among the requests for passing a public competition. Moreover, other criteria might prevent migrant women from working in their field once they have succeeded in the competitive exam. In this regard, I highlighted that Rosella, who was born in the DRC and succeeded in the competitive exam to become a physician in Italy, was shocked to learn that non-EU citizens could not register with the Italian medical association. Fortunately for Rosella, the norm was revoked, she could then register with the medical association and start working as a physician.

Attempting to Remove Barriers

The third group of employment strategies consists of removing obstacles that prevent migrant women from accessing jobs. Following this path has ambivalent consequences in terms of reproducing or challenging stratifications: on the one hand, these strategies imply that women accept that their foreign degrees are worth less or that local citizenship is needed to access graduate jobs; on the other hand, they can eventually facilitate migrant women's access to positions more in line with their studies.

Applying for Citizenship Not holding local citizenship can have several implications in limiting access to graduate positions. As mentioned, some posts or professional associations can be closed to foreigners. Moreover, local legislation might discourage the hiring of non-EU citizens. For instance, it was mentioned that in France, norms tend to discourage the recruitment and selection of non-EU citizens. Indeed employers that want to hire them have to pay a specific tax and have additional paperwork. As a result, migrant women might start the procedure to acquire local citizenship in order to have better access to graduate positions.

It emerged from my fieldwork that migrant women could feel puzzled when asking for local citizenship, as it could involve that they had to resign from the nationality they had at birth. As a result, they were postponing the request for local citizenship, as they did not want to be foreigners in their country of birth. An example that illustrates how migrant women can feel when faced with the risk of losing their nationality at birth was provided by Amapola, who was born in Albania and worked as an administrative assistant in France.

> *What I found reassuring is that I was able to keep my Albanian nationality. I didn't have to give it up. I admit that it would have hurt me a lot if I had to... I know that it's only at the level of papers, you can't change a person, but the fact of not having [Albanian] papers that [say that] I also belong to the country where I was born and where I have spent a large part of my life, I don't know, that would have been difficult. But I did [apply for French citizenship] without any fear because I knew I could keep both.* (Amapola, born in Albania, administrative assistant, France).

Women who were couples with Italian or French partners also brought to light another reason that restrained them from applying for local citizenship. Interviewees referred to the stigmatisation of migrant women that considered them as being *playgirls* or looking for a marriage of convenience. In this regard, Toffanin (2015) has highlighted that the representation of the ideal "romantic" love can be activated in a discriminatory way to stigmatise migrant women who are perceived as damaging the gratuitousness of love with instrumental considerations. In my fieldwork, Veronica, who was born in Ukraine and lived in Italy, indicated that she was puzzled about asking for Italian citizenship. She did not want it to seem that she had married to obtain that nationality.

> *In Ukraine, they would ask me "So, you married a rich old man". Instead, here in Italy, they were asking my husband "Oh, you married a Ukrainian girl so she must be a charming girl." And so, that was it...* (Veronica, born in Ukraine, business manager, Italy).

Moreover, although obtaining local citizenship might remove some barriers, it might not necessarily enable women to have equal access to graduate jobs, as compared to locals. An analogy can be drawn with Fassin's (2006) observations on undocumented migrants who are looking forward to getting a residence permit. According to the researcher, when these migrants end up being given a residence permit, they go through a phase of euphoria, and then quickly enter a period of disappointment: "it was not just the lack of a residence permit that penalised them" (Fassin, 2006: 145). Similarly, not having local citizenship is not the only obstacle that migrant women face when intending to access graduated jobs. It emerged from fieldwork interviews that migrant women were aware of such a limit. For instance, in France, Azalea was considering applying for French citizenship, but she was quite sceptical regarding the extent to which it would change her access to graduate jobs.

> *I always thought I could find something in French companies, which was definitely not the case. And actually, I hope to apply for citizenship next year. [But] I have very, very low hope of being hired by French companies. Even though there will be no problem with [my] documents, I still see that foreigners are seen less favourably, I would say.* (Azalea, born in Russia, administrative assistant, France).

Enrolling Again in Tertiary Education When migrant women become aware that their foreign degrees are not recognised in the country where they have migrated, they might decide to enrol again in tertiary education in order to obtain a local diploma. This path was undertaken by several of the women who were interviewed in my fieldwork. It implies that migrant women count on specific economic, social and cultural capital. Indeed, if they lack financial support, migrant women might engage in any job, postponing the moment in which re-enrolling in education.

In a few cases, women who already had significant working experience in their country of immigration requested to have local training funded by their employers, in the context of lifelong learning. This modality was identified in the French context. For instance, Callaia, who was born in Niger, enrolled again in education after working for several years as a nursing assistant in maternity in Alsace. She managed to have her training funded by her employer. As a result, she continued receiving her salary while studying at nursing school.

And since it was an [approved] training, they call it lifelong learning. The hospital that is my employer supports it. [...] So, they agreed to pay me while I was in training. [...] Well, it was a lot simpler to work and get paid than to... (laughs). I needed that salary. (Callaia, born in Niger, nurse, France).

It is worth noting that a consistent portion of interviewees did study in Italy and France, but was not finding employment in their fields. Similarly to the trend that was highlighted regarding the limits of accessing local citizenship, obtaining an Italian or French degree did not guarantee equal access to jobs compared to locals. Other criteria are at play, including the essentialist processes that were highlighted throughout this book. As mentioned, the frustration of not accessing graduate jobs, despite holding a local university degree was stressed by several interviewees.

Surfing Stratifications

Accessing positions in which migrant women are overrepresented can be perceived as a path that reproduces the existing stratifications of the labour market (Tognetti Bordogna, 2012). However, it might also correspond to strategies implemented by migrant women to access more rewarding positions. Rather than passively accepting employment stratifications, women who implement these strategies might *surf* these processes, meaning that they use them to their advantage.

Working with the 'Migrant Identity' One of the migrant women's paths to employment identified by Liversage (2009: 132) concerns the fact of gaining work based on the *migrant identity*. I propose to enlarge Liversage's (2009) definition of these jobs, so as to include all the positions in which migrant women can argue that they are more qualified than locals, based on effective or alleged skills they have acquired in their country of birth or through their experience as migrants. These are positions for which recruiters might look for candidates with specific linguistic skills or presume that there is cultural proximity with users or partners, such as in the social work sector (De Rudder & Vourc'h, 2006: 182), as already highlighted in Chap. 4.

It emerged from my fieldwork that accessing positions connected to the migrant identity can be part of a broader strategy to access employment more in line with migrant women's aspirations. Indeed, being employed as a cultural mediator or an export manager may work as a gateway to enter a company or a sector. Subsequently, migrant women might see their responsibilities increased and access jobs that are no longer strictly related to their migrant identity. An example was provided by Rada, who was born in Cameroon and graduated in Human Rights law in Italy. The woman started working in an NGO as a cultural mediator and ended up carrying out tasks similar to that of a social worker. Although her job still involved interacting with migrants, Rada's responsibilities at work had increased, and her tasks were not limited anymore to linguistic and cultural mediation.

> *So as a result, I was called from time to time to mediate here [at the workplace], or at the hospital, or at Questura [police headquarters], so I was still active. It's true, I did not have a fixed job, but I was active in one way or another. And so, after there was… the [cooperative] opened a new project […]. And so, they needed staff and they called me. And that's when I had [my] first contract with them.* (Rada, born in Cameroon, social worker, Italy).

When it comes to export management, migrant women tended to be hired at first to trade in their mother tongue or with the linguistic area connected to their country of birth. However, it happened that subsequently, they were asked to manage the trade with other areas and to perform tasks of business management that exceed interacting with foreign partners. An example was provided by Veronica, who was born in Ukraine and obtained a PhD in economics in Italy. Veronica initially worked in Veneto as a project manager to support the export trade of Italian companies in countries of the former Soviet Union. Little by little, Veronica started working with other areas, including China, Brazil, Singapore, and Dubai. After ten years of working in that field, she was in charge of business administration in a private company. Veronica started in a position connected to her migrant identity and progressively moved to graduate jobs that did not strictly connect to her migrant background.

> *I worked as a project manager. This company dealt with… they were consultants for micro, small, medium-sized Italian companies that wanted to export abroad. Most of it was with the ex-Soviet Union, then I was in charge of*

> *China, then I was in charge of Brazil, and Singapore, and Dubai. [...] Since January of this year, I have changed. I work for another company that deals with [name of product]. [...] I do quite different things: administration, even staff management, a bit of everything. It's a small company that is growing, and so there are so many things to do at the beginning.* (Veronica, born in Ukraine, business manager, Italy).

Overall, the strategy that consists of entering a company through a position connected to one's migrant identity and then accessing other jobs, brings to light that migrant women are also surfing representations and essentialism in order to make a career and access jobs more in line with their background.

Undertaking Vocational Training Migrant women might also use their knowledge of stratifications to implement other strategies that aim at surfing stratifications to obtain more rewarding positions. A second strategy that goes in this sense consists of undertaking vocational or informal training at work in order to access jobs that are still racialised and feminised but slightly more rewarding than entry-level positions. An example was provided by Rosanna, who was born in Cameroon and lived in Italy. Although she graduated in economics in Italy, she did not find employment in her field. As a result, Rosanna started working as an in-home carer. The woman strategically decided to undertake vocational training connected to her job so as to access positions more stable and rewarding than entry-level positions. More specifically, Rosanna took vocational training which permitted her to access the position of care assistant, which was better rewarded than that of an in-home carer.

> *As a result, I inquired about the training programme for care assistants. I enrolled in the programme. I was simultaneously following the lectures [in economics] at the university as they were no longer demanding. And I also passed this programme at the end of 2013.[...] I already had my fellow co-nationals who had finished economics, and other things at the university and who didn't, couldn't find work [...] I said to myself "I better have an extra card to play, and so if I can't find work with my degree, maybe with this diploma [I will]". Indeed I can say that it is what has given me work since then. From 2015 until now, it is my care assistant certificate. Because with my degree [in economics], I have never found a job.* (Rosanna, born in Cameroon, care assistant, Italy).

Migrant women that follow this path do not necessarily enrol in formal training. They might also find a way to informally acquire skills at work that enable them to access better positions. An example was that of Winika who was born in Ukraine and lived in Italy. She used to work as a waitress in the hospitality industry. However, she felt that "so many people" could do the work she was doing. As she wanted to gain skills that would give her access to a more secure job, she started learning how to make pizzas. Winika did not undertake formal training but acquired the skills at work. Thanks to her new ability, she managed to be hired as a pizza maker in another company.

> *I understood that I needed something regular, that there are so many people who can come to clean the table, I needed a job that would give me the security to stay at that place. So I learned to make pizzas. I became a pizzaiola [pizza maker]. That's where I became… Gimmicks, which allowed me to learn. Because you occupy a post, it is not that they allow you during working hours to give up your post and learn something nearby, even though you [only] need 2 minutes. I made gimmicks to learn.* (Winika, born in Ukraine, pizza maker, Italy).

Both cases, that of Rosanna and Winika, illustrate how migrant women use their knowledge of the labour market to surf stratifications and access positions that they perceived as more stable or rewarding. Thanks to vocational training, Rosanna managed to work as a care assistant rather than an in-home carer, while Winika used "gimmicks" to learn how to make pizzas and work as a *pizzaiola*. Although these strategies permitted them to access more stable and rewarding jobs than entry-level positions, both women felt frustrated for being inserted in stratified labour markets that gave no value to their academic titles.

* * *

Overall, after studying in the previous chapters how local labour markets are stratified and influenced by essentialism, this chapter has analysed how migrant women with tertiary education react to this twin phenomenon. In contrast with the representation that sees them as vulnerable victims (Parolari, 2019), the chapter has emphasised their *agency* when faced with essentialism and stratifications. The first section illustrated how migrant women cope, resist and eventually challenge essentialism.

The second section studied the strategies that are implemented to cope with labour market stratifications and access employment.

Throughout the chapter, it was stressed that gender, class, and eventually identities defined in terms of citizenship, country of birth or 'culture', interacted to cope with essentialism and stratifications. Moreover, it appeared that while some coping strategies reproduce forms of essentialism and employment stratifications, others aim at resisting and challenging them. Overall, I have highlighted that migrant women's everyday resistance practices and employment strategies that look to avoid confinement in jobs with low social recognition contribute to challenging and reconfiguring the stratifications of the local labour market. By implementing these practices and strategies, migrant women with tertiary education also contribute to decolonising imaginaries (Vergès, 2019).

References

Alberti, G. (2014). Mobility strategies,'mobility differentials' and 'transnational exit': the experiences of precarious migrants in London's hospitality jobs. *Work, Employment and Society, 28*(6), 865–881.

Allport, G. W. (1979). *The nature of prejudice.* Unabridged.

Bourdieu, P. (1986). The forms of capital. *Cultural Theory: An Anthology, 1*(2011), 81–93.

Collins, P. H. (2000). *Black feminist thought – Knowledge, consciousness and the politics of empowerment.* Routledge.

De Rudder, V., & Vourc'h, F. (2006). Les discriminations racistes dans le monde du travail. In D. Fassin & E. Fassin (Eds.), *De la question sociale à la question raciale ? Représenter la société française.* La Découverte.

Eijberts, M., & Roggeband, C. (2016). Stuck with the stigma? How Muslim migrant women in the Netherlands deal–individually and collectively–with negative stereotypes. *Ethnicities, 16*(1), 130–153.

Faggian, A., Rose Olfert, M., & Partridge, M. D. (2011). Inferring regional well-being from individual revealed preferences: The 'voting with your feet' approach. *Cambridge Journal of Regions, Economy and Society, 5*(1), 163–180.

Fassin, D. (2006). Du déni à la dénégation. Psychologie politique de la représentation des discriminations. In D. Fassin & E. Fassin (Eds.), *De la question sociale à la question raciale ? Représenter la société française* (pp. 133–157). La Découverte.

Goffman, E. (1990). *Stigma.Notes on the management of spoiled identity*. Penguin.
Gussow, Z., & Tracy, G. (1968). Status, ideology, and adaptation to stigmatized illness: A study of leprosy. *Human Organization, 27*(4), 316–325.
Hochschild, A. R. (2012). *The managed heart: Commercialization of human feeling*. University of California Press.
Killian, C., & Manohar, N. N. (2015). Highly skilled immigrant Women's labor market access. *Social Currents, 3*(2), 138–159.
Kofman, E., & Raghuram, P. (2015). *Gendered migrations and global social reproduction*. Palgrave Macmillan UK.
Lancee, B. (2012). The economic returns of bonding and bridging social capital for immigrant men in Germany. *Ethnic and Racial Studies., 35*(4), 664–683.
Liversage, A. (2009). Vital conjunctures, shifting horizons: High-skilled female immigrants looking for work. *Work, Employment & Society, 23*(1), 120–141.
Lyon, D. (2006). The organization of care work in Italy: Gender and migrant labor in the new economy. *Indiana Journal of Global Legal Studies, 13*(1), 207–224.
Miller, C. T., & Kaiser, C. R. (2001). A theoretical perspective on coping with stigma. *Journal of Social Issues., 57*(1), 73–92.
Moroşanu, L. (2016). Professional bridges: Migrants' ties with natives and occupational advancement. *Sociology, 50*(2), 349–365. https://doi.org/10.1177/0038038514568234
Moroşanu, L., & Fox, J. E. (2013). 'No smoke without fire': Strategies of coping with stigmatised migrant identities. *Ethnicities, 13*(4), 438–456.
Parolari, P. (2019). Stereotipi di genere, discriminazioni contro le donne e vulnerabilità come disempowerment. Riflessioni sul ruolo del diritto. *About Gender, 8*(15), 90–117.
Portes, A., & Bach, R. L. (1985). *Latin journey: Cuban and Mexican immigrants in the United States*. University of California Press.
Riessman, C. K. (2000). Stigma and everyday resistance practices: Childless women in South India. *Gender & Society, 14*(1), 111–135.
Toffanin, A. M. (2015). *Controcanto. Donne latinoamericane tra violenza e riconoscimento*. Guerini Scientifica.
Tognetti Bordogna, M. (2012). *Donne e percorsi migratori*. Franco Angeli.
Vergès, F. (2019). *Un féminisme décolonial*. La Fabrique.
Vianello, F. A. (2014). Ukrainian migrant workers in Italy: Coping with and reacting to downward mobility. *Central and eastern European Migration Review, 3*(1), 85–98.
Wacquant, L. (2008). *Urban outcasts: A comparative sociology of advanced marginality*. Polity Press.

6

"Maybe This Will Be Useful for the Future". Expanding Research on Essentialism

Winika, who was born in Ukraine and worked as a pizza maker in Italy, gave me an appointment in front of her university to meet for the interview. The woman had recently enrolled in a graduate program after years of being out of academia. Once we greeted each other and introduced ourselves, we agreed to move away from the university and look for a place where we could talk a little further away from indiscreet ears. In the end, we decided to sit at the riverside, where we discussed her situation and interest in the topic for more than an hour. When I turned on the recorder, after asking her permission, Winika was about to share her intimate life and thoughts with a person she had never met before. This woman had plenty of questions about my research and specified:

> *I'm asking you because I liked the research topic, and maybe this will be useful for the future. That is why I immediately said yes, without even thinking that much about it, because I liked the idea. (Winika, born in Ukraine, pizza maker, Italy).*

Echoing Winika's comment, we could wonder what the worth of this research is. What is its contribution to the literature and how can it be "useful for the future"? After five chapters and hundreds of pages of

A.-I. Romens, *Deconstructing Essentialism*,
https://doi.org/10.1007/978-3-031-14399-1_6

analysis, fragments of life and feelings, that have touched upon a variety of complex issues regarding stratifications and essentialism in the labour markets, the following pages have the aim of summarising the crucial points that emerged from the study, highlighting its contribution to the debate on migrants' access to employment and identifying paths to guarantee more equal access to jobs.

When I started drafting the research project that served as a basis for writing the book, I was unsure about the extent to which I would be able to grasp how essentialism matters when accessing jobs. However, after my first interviews, I had the confirmation that, although essentialism is an understudied issue when it comes to analysing migrant women's access to employment, it is crucial to understand their working trajectories. Through conducting narrative interviews and crossing the perspectives of different actors, it was possible to stress the complex mechanisms that contribute to reproducing stratifications (Yuval-Davis, 2015) and highlight the influence of essentialism in this process.

Multisiting research permitted me to contextualise the phenomena (Bloemraad, 2013), highlighting similarities and differences in the way essentialism impacts access to jobs depending on how gender, racialisation and migration regimes intersect at the local level. When it comes to similarities, in both countries, research participants referred to essentialist beliefs based on gender, class, and racialisation that associated migrant women with characteristics that were appreciated or disdained by recruiters. Both in Alsace and Veneto, Black migrant women were particularly exposed to racialisation, although migrant women from Eastern European countries were also targeted by *othering* and essentialism. These findings permitted me to complete previous research and stress that essentialism in recruitment and selection does not only concern jobs with low social recognition, but also influences access to jobs throughout the employment structure.

My research also highlights differences in the way essentialism impacts access to jobs depending on the context. For instance, in Italy research participants mentioned complex stratifications of the labour market and provided elaborate descriptions of how essentialism based on gender, racialisation, and class influences the selection and recruitment process, highlighting that essentialist criteria can be explicitly used by recruiters and employers. Although essentialism has a role to play in the access to jobs in France as well, stratifications based on nationality and racialisation appeared to be less explicit and participants rather emphasised the opposition between migrants and non-migrants. The difference between the two contexts was connected to the different models of addressing migrants' otherness.

By using an analytical lens that aimed at deconstructing essentialist discourses, it was possible to deepen the analysis and study how essentialism influences the way recruiters perceive education and experience gained abroad, as well as language, and soft skills. It appeared that skills assessment is influenced by essentialist representations based on global hierarchies and colonial imaginaries (Grosfoguel et al., 2015) that intersect gender, class, and racialisation. In this regard, the analysis made it possible to highlight that skills are embodied, meaning that they are valued according to how recruiters perceive the person that holds them.

The study also permitted me to highlight the *agency* of migrant women and labour market gatekeepers. In doing so, I contrasted the representations that see, on the one hand, migrant women as passive victims of essentialism (Parolari, 2019; Rosenthal et al., 2020) and, on the other hand, recruiters and social workers as passively reproducing labour market essentialist mechanisms (Alberti & Iannuzzi, 2020). When it comes to migrant women, I identified a series of strategies that they implement to cope, resist and eventually challenge essentialism, which permitted me to complete existing typologies of coping strategies (Eijberts & Roggeband, 2016; Rosenthal et al., 2020; Hametner et al., 2020). As far as recruiters and social workers are concerned, I have stressed that through their practices and depending on the extent to which they perceive that they have margins of action, they might reproduce or eventually challenge essentialism and stratifications.

To complete the analysis of the book, future research is needed to explore how essentialist representations vary according to recruiters' characteristics and trajectories. Indeed, we could wonder how recruiters' gender, class, migratory background and experience of being essentialised influence their perception of migrant women and the way they assess their skills. To go further, it would also be interesting to analyse how essentialism conditions access to other resources and rights. For instance, besides employment, we could wonder how essentialism also limits migrant women's access to housing, training, health services and social rights, among others.

In addition to contributing to the scholarly debate on migrant women's access to employment, the book also aims at providing food for thought to the reader to identify levers on which pressure can be put to guarantee more equal access to jobs. Through its in-depth description of the mechanisms that contribute to reproducing inequalities in the labour market, the analysis has highlighted some of the specific barriers that prevent migrant women from accessing employment. In this regard, international treaty bodies and commissions have emphasised the need to remove such obstacles. For instance, the United Nations Committee on the Elimination of Discrimination against Women (CEDAW, 2008) and the European Commission against Racism and Intolerance (ECRI, 2012) have recently published recommendations to their member states, including Italy and France, in which they request governments to take steps to ensure that migrant women have equal access to employment. More specifically, the CEDAW (2008) calls for "lifting discriminatory bans or restrictions on immigration", including visa schemes that indirectly discriminate against migrant women.

My study has brought to light some of the specific legal constraints that lead to unequal access to employment. For instance, I stressed that restrictive family reunification policies are repelling recruiters from hiring migrant women as they fear short-term permits will not be renewed. Research participants also referred to the laws that introduce additional paperwork or taxes for employers who wish to hire non-European foreigners, such as the mechanisms described by Azalea in my French fieldwork (see Chap. 3). I also stressed that jobs in the public sector or those regulated by professional associations might exclude migrant women, creating double standards, in which migrant women are treated as second-class workers, such as in the case of health professionals employed in Italian subcontracting cooperatives (see Chap. 3).

Besides removing specific legal barriers, the analysis of the book has stressed that there is a broader need to transform essentialist representations of migrant women and *decolonise imaginaries* (Vergès, 2019), which implies tackling racism, sexism and other forms of oppression that connect to essentialism. This long-term objective involves, among other issues, recognising past and current colonisation, and how it influences social relations and stratifications of the labour market. However, researchers have stressed that gender, class, and racialised hierarchies are functional for economic interests (Tsing, 2009), as they permit employers to reduce labour costs, legitimising forms of labour exploitation and making invisible the efforts that subaltern workers put into performing their job. Consequently, the desire to transform these mechanisms risks facing many resistances. Moreover, as long as there will be relations of domination and colonialism, global inequalities will likely continue to be reflected at the local level, through stratifications and unequal access to employment and resources (Bonilla Silva, 2014; Grosfoguel et al., 2015).

Therefore, although international human rights mechanisms have expressed a growing interest regarding the discriminations faced by migrant women when accessing jobs, there is a tension between their declarations of principles, on the one side, and the political and economic interests at the local, national and international level that promote excluding migration regimes (Mezzadra & Neilson, 2013), on the other side. For instance, guaranteeing equality between migrants and non-migrants has been far from being among political priorities in recent years in France and Italy. In both countries, several NGOs and independent institutions have criticised the hardening of migratory policies, which have reached a "new low" in Italy - according to Human Rights Watch (2018) - and reinforced the acceptance of seeing migrants being treated differently in France - according to the French Commissioner for Human Rights (Le Défenseur des Droits, 2016).

Nevertheless, during the same period, lawsuits brought by migrant workers and civil society associations have made it possible to widen access to public employment for migrants in Italy (ASGI, 2017) and to make systemic racial discrimination recognised in France (GISTI, 2020). Moreover, the self-organised movements driven by migrant women workers, such as that of the hotel maids in Paris who succeeded after 22 months of struggle to sign an agreement with their employer in May 2021 (Amnesty International, 2021) and the multiple civil society initiatives that aim at supporting migrants in accessing rights, illustrate that there is also a wish to build counter-narratives and guarantee migrants equal access to employment. These movements reflect the tensions that exist in European societies, but also emphasise that other paths can be undertaken, adopting policies that ensure migrant women have equal access to resources and rights.

References

Alberti, G., & Iannuzzi, F. E. (2020). Embodied intersectionality and the intersectional management of hotel labour: The everyday experiences of social differentiation in customer-oriented work. *Gender, Work and Organization, 27*(6), 1165–1180.

Amnesty International. (2021). *Femmes de ménage : les dernières de cordée se rebiffent*. Available at: https://www.amnesty.fr/actualites/femmes-de-menage%2D%2Dles-dernieres-de-cordee-se-rebiffent

Asgi. (2017). «Tribunale di Firenze, ordinanza 27 maggio 2017», 27/05/2017. Available at: https://www.asgi.it/banca-dati/tribunale-firenze-ordinanza-27-maggio-2017/

Bloemraad, I. (2013). The promise and pitfalls of comparative research design in the study of migration. *Migration Studies, 1*(1), 27–46.

Bonilla Silva, E. (2014). *Racism without racists*. Rowman & Littlefield.

CEDAW. (2008). General recommendation no. 26 on women migrant workers, CEDAW/C/2009/WP.1/R.

ECRI. (2012). General policy recommendation no. 14 on combating racism and racial discrimination in employment, CRI(2012)48.

Eijberts, M., & Roggeband, C. (2016). Stuck with the stigma? How Muslim migrant women in the Netherlands deal–individually and collectively–with negative stereotypes. *Ethnicities, 16*(1), 130–153.

Gisti. (2020). Les discriminations raciales systémiques enfin condamnées, *Plein droit* n° 124, mars 2020.

Grosfoguel, R., Oso, L., & Christou, A. (2015). Racism, intersectionality and migration studies: Framing some theoretical reflections. *Identities: Global Studies in Culture and Power, 22*(6), 635–652.

Hametner, K., Rodax, N., Steinicke, K., & McQuarrie, J. (2020). 'After all, I have to show that I'm not different': Muslim women's psychological coping strategies with dichotomous and dichotomising stereotypes. *European Journal of Women's Studies, 28*(1), 56–70.

Human Rights Watch. (2018, September 26). *New low for Italian migration policies. Preventing Rescue at sea, punishing survivors on land.* Available at https://www.hrw.org/news/2018/09/26/new-low-italian-migration-policies
Le Défenseur des Droits. (2016, May). *Les droits fondamentaux des étrangers en France.* Available at: https://www.defenseurdesdroits.fr/sites/default/files/atoms/files/736160170_ddd_rapport_droits_etrangers.pdf
Mezzadra, S., & Neilson, B. (2013). *Border as method, or, the multiplication of labor*. Duke University Press.
Parolari, P. (2019). Stereotipi di genere, discriminazioni contro le donne e vulnerabilità come disempowerment. Riflessioni sul ruolo del diritto. *About Gender, 8*(15), 90–117.
Rosenthal, L., Overstreet, N. M., Khukhlovich, A., Brown, B. E., Godfrey, C.-J., & Albritton, T. (2020). Content of, sources of, and responses to sexual stereotypes of black and Latinx women and men in the United States: A qualitative intersectional exploration. *Journal of Social Issues, 76*(4), 921–948.
Tsing, A. (2009). Supply chains and the human condition. *Rethinking Marxism, 21*(2), 148–176.
Vergès, F. (2019). *Un féminisme décolonial.* La Fabrique éditions.
Yuval-Davis, N. (2015). Situated intersectionality and social inequality. *Raisons Politiques, 58*(2), 91–100.

Index[1]

[1] Note: Page numbers followed by 'n' refer to notes.

A.-I. Romens, *Deconstructing Essentialism*,
https://doi.org/10.1007/978-3-031-14399-1